PAPERBOY

A MEMOIR

# BIOGRAPHY

Tony Macaulay grew up at the top of the Shankill Road in Belfast. This experience has shaped his life. Tony has spent the past 25 years working to build peace and reconciliation at home and abroad. In the 1990s he developed and implemented local and international youth programmes on conflict resolution. In 2008, following his experience of living on and working on the peace lines, he developed a discussion paper proposing a process for the removal of the 'peace walls' in Northern Ireland.

Tony is also a writer and broadcaster and has been a regular contributor to BBC Radio Ulster. He married Lesley in 1986 and they have two children, Beth and Hope. *Paperboy* is his first book.

To Ellen

A MEMOIR

Best wishes

Tony Macaulay

Tony x

Thanks for all your hard work
to build peace in Northern
Ireland!

MERLIN
PUBLISHING

First published in 2010 by Merlin Publishing
Newmarket Hall, Cork Street
Dublin 8, Ireland
Tel: +353 1 453 5866
Fax: +353 1 453 5930
publishing@merlin.ie
www.merlinwolfhound.com
Text © 2010 Tony Macaulay
Editing, Design and Layout © 2010 Merlin Publishing

ISBN 978-1907162-05-3

A CIP catalogue record for this book is available from the British Library.

10 9 8 7 6 5 4 3 2 1

Typeset by Merlin Publishing
Cover design by Graham Thew Design
Cover image courtesy of the *Belfast Telegraph*
Printed and bound by CPI Cox & Wyman, Britain

**Disclaimer: Some names and identifying details have been changed to protect the privacy of individuals.**

# DEDICATION

This book is dedicated to my parents, Betty and Eric Macaulay, their good friends, Ella and Harry Maguire, and all the voluntary youth leaders who kept young people off the streets and safe in Belfast in the 1970s. They are the unsung heroes of the Troubles.

# ACKNOWLEDGEMENTS

Ever since I was a boy I've had dreams of writing a book.

Even when I was a paperboy up the Shankill in 1975, I daydreamed that one day a book would be published with my name on the front. To be perfectly honest, the dream was that the book would be an explosive science-fiction classic, with silver robots on the front cover, that would be made into a Hollywood blockbuster movie to rival *Star Wars*! I never imagined back then that one day my dream would come true, or that the book would simply be about being a paperboy up the Shankill in 1975.

So, as you can imagine, I am enormously grateful to everyone who helped to make that wee boy's dream come true.

I will always be thankful for a happy childhood, for a loving family and good friends.

I especially want to express appreciation to my wife and soul mate, Lesley, for listening patiently to every word of every draft. I also want to thank my daughters, Beth and Hope, for demonstrating great tolerance while their dad was going on and on about what they call 'the olden days'.

I want to acknowledge Susan Feldstein's experience and remarkable skill, which she applied with great support and positivity, throughout the editing phase. I throughly enjoyed the process and learned a great deal about good writing.

Finally, I want to thank Chenile Keogh and Robert Doran from Merlin Publishing for believing in *Paperboy*, for all their hard work and warm encouragement and for working their magic to make my dream come true.

# CONTENTS

| | | |
|---|---|---|
| *Introduction* | | xi |
| *Chapter One* | Recruitment and Induction | 13 |
| *Chapter Two* | Hoods and Robbers | 25 |
| *Chapter Three* | The Belfast Crack | 37 |
| *Chapter Four* | Secrets at School | 53 |
| *Chapter Five* | A Rival Arrives | 67 |
| *Chapter Six* | Three Steps to Heaven | 83 |
| *Chapter Seven* | Tips and Investments | 97 |
| *Chapter Eight* | Good Livin' | 111 |
| *Chapter Nine* | Wider Horizons | 125 |
| *Chapter Ten* | Paper Mum | 139 |
| *Chapter Eleven* | Scouts, Bombs and Bullets | 149 |
| *Chapter Twelve* | A Final Verbal Warning | 159 |
| *Chapter Thirteen* | Sharing Streets with Soldiers | 179 |
| *Chapter Fourteen* | Save the Children | 193 |
| *Chapter Fifteen* | Peace in the Papers | 209 |
| *Chapter Sixteen* | Puppy Love | 223 |
| *Chapter Seventeen* | Musical Distractions | 235 |
| *Chapter Eighteen* | Across the Walls | 251 |
| *Chapter Nineteen* | Winners | 261 |
| *Chapter Twenty* | The Last Round | 277 |

# INTRODUCTION

I was a paperboy. This never made it to my CV. So, just for the record, the dates of employment were 1975–1977. The place was Belfast.

I delivered the evening *Belfast Telegraph* — forty-eight *Belly Tellys* each night in the darkness. Belfast in the seventies was like the newspapers I delivered. Everything was black and white, albeit Orange and Green. Everything got smudged and ruined, like dark ink from the stories that dirtied my hands every day. But there were chinks of colour too, like in the weekly glossy magazines I provided to the more affluent customers of the Upper Shankill.

I was a paperboy. Aged twelve. Thin and easily crumpled. Blown around the streets by greater forces. More smart than tough. Yearning for peace, but living through Troubles.

And yet, as you will learn in these slightly less fragile pages, I was happy with my calling. I was a good paperboy. I delivered.

# CHAPTER ONE

## *recruitment and induction*

I was too young, so I was. You had to be a teenager to be a paperboy for Oul' Mac. He gave my big brother the paper round in our street when he was thirteen. By the time I was twelve, I was jealous of the money and the status. I couldn't wait an extra year to get my foot on this first rung of the employment ladder. So one wet Belfast night, I persuaded my brother to introduce me to Oul' Mac and to inform him of my desire to enter his employment.

My first job interview was a nerve-wracking experience.

'Have you any rounds going, Mr Mac?' I asked. (You never called him Oul' to his face.)

'Aye, all right,' said Oul' Mac, 'but no thievin', or you're out!'

With this stipulation of the one essential criterion for the job, I concluded correctly that my application for the post had been successful. My prospective employer didn't even ask if I was thirteen yet, so I didn't have to tell lies. Lies were a sin back then.

So, at the age of twelve, I set out on my career as a paperboy. My fear of age exposure gradually dissolved as I approached my thirteenth birthday, when I became completely legit. I no longer had nightmares about being arrested by the RUC for underage paper delivery.

No sooner had I taken up my new position than my big brother decided that paper rounds were now only for wee kids and he summarily left the arena of newspaper delivery entirely to me. I did nothing to dissuade him. I was delighted. Now the papers would be my exclusive territory. My wee brother was still more interested in Lego and Milky Bars and *Watch with Mother*, but I could sense that he envied my new career and was longing for the day when he too could follow in the family tradition.

Oul' Mac liked me. He said I was a good, honest boy. This was important to him. It meant you wouldn't steal the paper money that you collected from the customers on a Friday evening. He was a tough boss, though. He sacked wee lads all the time. Half our street had been sacked by Oul' Mac. But if you did a good job, with no cheek to the pensioners and no thieving, he didn't shout at you much and your position was secure. I knew I had to learn these rules fast, since my whole career would depend on sticking to them.

Oul' Mac had been a newsagent on the Upper Shankill for decades: no one could remember anybody else ever delivering the papers up our way. But he was getting on a bit now. Oul' Mac smoked and said 'f**k' a lot. Of course, most men smoked and said 'f**k' a lot, but Oul' Mac did both, simultaneously and ceaselessly. He was a thin man with no beer belly to hold up his tatty trousers and so he was always hoisting them up, in between cigarette drags. I never saw him smile, but sometimes his eyes twinkled and I couldn't work out whether he was coughing or laughing. On these rare occasions when his mouth opened wide, I would worry for his last few wobbly, yellowing teeth, teetering on the brink of self-extraction.

Oul' Mac had dark yellow fingers, where the nicotine of ten thousand cigarettes blended with the printing ink of a million newspapers. His skin was dark and leathery, because he was outdoors most of the time, filling and emptying his van. His face and arms were also of a yellowy hue. Mrs Mac said he was bad with his liver. He had only a few remaining tufts of hair, white and in places the same dark yellow as his stained hands. This hair always stood upright, gelled in place by the binding glue of a million magazines on his fingers.

Our distinguished newsagent baron's van had also seen better times. It was the same shade of dirty yellow as his hair and nails, apart from the rusty red bits around the bottom that sometimes fell off when it went over security ramps. This van spluttered around our puddled streets every day, the exhaust pipe just about hanging in there. Whenever you went outside, Oul' Mac's Ford Transit was always there on the street, like dogs and marbles and soldiers.

Following my appointment to the post of paperboy, I would wait every night for this legendary vehicle at the end of our street. You heard the roar as it struggled up the hill in the distance, sounding like some part might drop off at any moment, in the titanic struggle between gravity, tons of paper and the failing power of an ageing Ford Transit engine. But Mac always made it, even in the snow when you hoped he wouldn't, so you could have snowball fights with the other paperboys. Even through the barricades, when you feared his temper might get him hurt, as he told the paramilitaries to f**k off and give his head peace.

Often the papers were late and the reason was right there in the headlines – dark words on grey pages. I seldom read the *Belfast Telegraph*, though. It was full of charmless men talking about 'them and us', and depressing bombs and killings, and why it was all the other side's fault and, sure, I was living in the middle of the whole thing anyway. I was more interested in tips and TV and bonfires and music and outer space and Sharon Burgess. Sharon Burgess was lovely. I fancied her, so I did. She was my first sweetheart. I wanted her to be my own personal Olivia Newton-John.

These were the tuneful times of Showaddywaddy and the tartan tones of the Bay City Rollers. The days of Dad enjoying the blonde one in Pan's People dancing on *Top of the Pops*, when the Osmonds from America were No.1 and couldn't get to the BBC in London, where Harold Wilson with the pipe was Prime Minister. Elvis was getting fatter and I was getting taller. They were days for me of painful, string-imprinted fingertips from learning the guitar and violin, and going to music lessons at the Belfast School of Music and singing in the youth club choir at Ballygomartin Presbyterian Church. I'd have to endure flute bands every Twelfth of July, but at least I loved the mysterious slapping of the Lambeg drums in the distance on warm summer nights.

This was the era of getting your first colour TV on hire purchase, complete with miraculous push buttons to switch between the three television channels. In *Blue Peter* on BBC 1, Valerie Singleton, John Noakes and Peter Purves showed me how to make an *Apollo* spacecraft from toilet rolls and silver milk-bottle tops. I wept when Freda, the *Blue Peter* tortoise didn't make it through the winter in a cardboard box held together by sticky back plastic.

Then came our first black-and-white portable TV, clunky and bright red, with a handle on top. My big brother would use it to watch *Little House on the Prairie* in secret in the sitting room. (Hard men were not supposed to care about the trials of Laura Ingalls.) Meanwhile, my wee brother would watch *Romper Room* on UTV, waiting excitedly for Miss Helen to see him through her magic mirror and say his name at the end of every programme. My granny kept a tally of Irish-sounding names, to check if Miss Helen was seeing more Catholics than Protestants.

My mother watched old people in a pub on *Coronation Street* on UTV, and fancied Tom Jones when he sang 'The Green Green Grass of Home' on BBC 1. The appeal of both was lost on me. I rarely pushed the BBC 2 button either, but my father did, and watched long documentaries and *Monty Python's Flying Circus*, laughing hysterically when the posh Englishmen wore dresses, talked in high-pitched voices and did silly walks. It was a time when the family was safe and happy, and everyone was still alive, apart from my other granda. It was before the Carlsberg Special and the tears.

Parallel trousers were the fashion statement to die for, and tartan turn-ups and trouser legs were savagely shortened to every shin on the Shankill. Platform shoes were all the rage, and you would sprain your ankle for the sake of style when you jumped a fence and landed awkwardly in dog's dirt after raiding old Mr Butler's orchard, even though your mother had told you to 'leave the poor oul' fella alone because he was bad with his nerves'. Women in widely flared trousers marched for peace, and soldiers in khaki uniforms, with guns and English accents, would have tea and freshly baked apple cream buns at Auntie Mabel's. It was the era of the balaclava, and strangely familiar men wearing dark glasses on the barricades. Every lamp post had a flag. Every kerbstone had a colour. It was supposedly a time for hate and a time for war with the other side, but I reserved my hatred for homework and my only war was with acne. The world was ruled by the I-R-A and the U-D-A, but I was under the spell of a less threatening acronym: A-B-B-A.

The Co-op Superstore in town was always on fire, while the chippy down the road was always open. Familiar smells were the hint of Tayto Cheese & Onion crisps on the breath, the whiff of vinegar from warm fish suppers in fresh newspapers, and an aromatic mix of Brut aftershave, Benson & Hedges cigarettes and burning double-decker buses which often hung heavy in the air.

It was the electrifying age of Doctor Who with the long scarf who travelled in the TARDIS through time and space to save the universe. The Thunderbirds blasted off from Tracy Island to save the world, and Ian Paisley shouted a lot down a microphone at the City Hall to save Ulster.

There were horrors — like bloody bits of people on the pavement at the shops, and dirty protests in the prisons. But my horror was doing the Eleven Plus in primary school. Yet there were moments of bliss too — sleeping in a bunk bed in the caravan, and getting saved beside the sea, and a first kiss from Big Ruby in the sand dunes on the County Down coast.

For Paperboy, those years followed a familiar pattern, punctuated by School Term, Summer Holidays, the

Eleventh Night, the Twelfth of July, Halloween and Christmas Day. The changing seasons diverted my attention from pencil sharpeners to candy floss, from flags and bonfires to sparklers and Santa. Every week followed a well-trodden path too, like an experienced paperboy doing his rounds. School started again every Monday, Scouts was on Wednesdays, *Top of the Pops* was on Thursdays, the Europa Hotel got blown up on Fridays, the Westy Disco was on Saturdays, and on the seventh day I had to have a bath and go to Sunday school.

It was the seventies, all action-packed and fast-moving, like an episode of *Starsky and Hutch*. We had thirty-minute school classes and five-minute bomb warnings. One minute, I would be in the classroom learning about the transverse section of an earthworm and the next I was in the playground learning about girls and perfecting the lead guitar section of 'Bohemian Rhapsody'. If I wasn't being good by having a jumble sale for the Biafran babies or going to 'wee meetin's' to sing songs about Jesus, then I was being bad by bullying a wee ginger boy with National Health glasses or going to discos with rock-and-roll songs about sex and drugs and other things I didn't know how to do.

However, as soon as I was employed, all of these distractions melted into the background of my existence. Once I answered my calling, being a paperboy took top priority. I took my new-found profession very seriously. It was my vocation, so it was. Oul' Mac had discovered me. He had entrusted me with a great responsibility, and I was determined to fulfill the potential he had clearly discerned from my candid blue eyes, skinny four-foot frame and stringy straight black hair.

Every night, when Oul' Mac arrived in our street with the papers, he would fling open the double doors at the back of the van and jump up inside to dispense both papers and judgement. We paperboys held our collective breath. This was Oul' Mac's stage, and if a customer had complained or if your paper money hadn't added up, a gritty drama would unfold. I witnessed several summary sackings at the van doors, when the guilty faced the humiliation of having to hand over their paperbags in front of their former colleagues. Oul' Mac would snatch the bag roughly from the dirty-handed guilty one, who would then run down the street, telling him where he could stick his paper round.

Your paperbag was an important tool of the trade. Actually, it was the only one. On my first day, I was handed a clean white canvas bag, strong enough to hold a hundred *Tellys*. As my career progressed, the ever-darkening colour of my bag was a testament to my level of experience as a paperboy.

On my first night Oul' Mac handed me a database of my customers. It was a list of street numbers scrawled on the back of one of the dirty wee paper sweetie bags he used for the humbugs he sold in the shop.

'This is my mission if I choose to accept it,' I thought, imagining I was an American spy being sent out on *Mission Impossible*. I followed the numbers on the dirty wee paper bag as seriously as any secret agent hoping to crack a code to stop evil Russians from trying to take over the world. I criss-crossed the streets between odd numbers and even numbers, identifying target letterboxes and then launching paper missiles through marked front doors.

Some customers had impressive shiny brass numbers screwed onto their front doors, while others had simply painted their house number on a gatepost with some white gloss paint left over from painting the skirting board in their hall. Some of the houses had lush botanical gardens, while others had paved over the grass to park a motorbike. I learned that some gates were there to keep dogs and small children in and must always be closed, while other gates were for impressing the neighbours or just for swinging on.

On my virgin paper round, I was tentative and careful, just feeling my way. It was my first time, so I jumped no fences and closed all gates. It took me a while to work out exactly how to fold each paper and insert it correctly into each letterbox.

I smiled at all customers, even those who scowled back, like Mr Black from No. 13, who felt compelled to comment: 'They'll be delivering your paper in a pram next!'

I paid attention to developing good customer relations from the outset. I met Mrs Grant from No. 2 at her front gate. She was just back from the shops with a bagful of pigs' trotters from the butchers and a prescription from the chemist for her Richard's throat. I opened her gate and offered to carry her shopping bags.

'Och, thank you, love,' she said, 'I'm late for the dinner and my Richard's in bed with his throat.'

'I'm the new paperboy,' I proclaimed proudly.

'Och, that's lovely, love, close the gate after you,' Mrs Grant replied.

I could tell we were going to have an excellent customer/ supplier relationship. My mind already drifted towards an assessment of Mrs Grant's tip potential. My big brother said the good tippers would tell you to keep the change, while the 'stingy bastards' would expect every last halfpenny, even at Christmas.

My first few papers were awkwardly folded and came a little torn around the edges, but by the time I had delivered my final *Belfast Telegraph* on that first night, I had become nearly competent. The last newspaper of the night was withdrawn from my paper bag, folded perfectly and delivered swiftly within a mere ten seconds.

As I bounced away from No. 102, I heard the door unbolt behind me and then the voice of Mrs Charlton with the Scottish accent calling: 'Och, that's great, love. Don't forget my *Sunday Post* – and will you bring my bin round the back on a Wednesday, and I'll give you 10p for a wee 99 from the poke man?!'

Mrs Charlton had 'good tipper' written all over her.

I knew already that I was going to be great at this. My hands were so black now that I could barely read the numbers listed on the dirty wee sweetie paper bag Oul' Mac had given me – yet I would need this source of vital information with me for the rest of the week, by which time I had committed all my odd and even numbers to memory. It was like learning algebra, but with a purpose.

When I got back to our house after my first paper round, my mother was in the living room on the sewing machine, making another dress for a swanky lady on the Malone Road. Mammy was always sewing for someone, and she had the very latest sewing machine from the Great Universal Club Book. It was so expensive she was allowed to pay it off over sixty weeks instead of the usual twenty.

'Well, how did it go, love?' she enquired.

'Aye, no probs!' I replied, clearly indicating a positive self-evaluation of my first day of paid employment.

'Was any of them oul' dolls cheeky to you?' she asked.

'No, Mammy, they were all dead on. Mrs Grant and yer Scotchy woman are going to give me a good tip, so they are, but Mr Black thinks I'm too young to be a paperboy,' I confided.

'Never mind that oul get,' Mammy said. 'Sure, he's too old himself to be anything!'

'Where's Daddy?' I asked.

'He's doin' overtime to pay for the new suite in the sitting room,' she explained. 'He thinks it's great you've got yourself a wee job now. He says no son of his will ever be working late in a foundry three nights a week.'

Every evening Oul' Mac would cut the white string which held the Sixth Edition *Belfast Telegraphs* tightly in a bulging batch, releasing forty-eight copies into my care. I would then fill my paperbag and sling it over my shoulder. At the start of the round, my shoulder ached, especially on Thursdays and Fridays, when the papers had extra pages, and the weekly colour magazines arrived. A bagful of *Belly Tellys* later, the lessening of the burden over my shoulder would be matched by a lightness of spirit and the realisation that my work for the day was almost done.

I received no formal induction into my job as a paperboy, but quickly enough I picked up the essential requirements of the position from the other wee lads. The basic rules were simple: always turn up, no thieving, no late delivery, close all gates behind you and no cheek. That was easy enough. I soon discovered however that there were some additional, more subtle dos and don'ts that were also part of the unwritten induction manual. But more of this later.

I did of course get distracted from my work at times. I was learning new skills, such as playing guitar like Paul McCartney and snogging at the Westy Disco. There were other exciting things happening in my life, like getting saved on a bin at the caravan and going to see the Bay City Rollers in concert at the Ulster Hall. I had my share of worries too, like my bad heart, secrets at school and the dangers of hoods and robbers and bullets.

Yet in spite of these distractions, I trod purposefully along my new career path. I soon learned the ropes and mastered the fences, and within six months, while all around me had been sacked, I was still there, proudly carrying a dirty grey paper bag over my shoulder when I arrived at Oul' Mac's van each evening.

# CHAPTER TWO

## *hoods and robbers*

I knew there were risks to being a paperboy, especially on shadowy Friday nights when you had to collect the paper money for Oul' Mac. The introduction of hard cash into the equation caused Fridays to be darker and more threatening than any other night of the week. Robbers were an occupational hazard, the main health-and-safety risk for a Shankill paperboy.

Other week nights, I was carefree. I would run down the street, slapping a folded newspaper all along Mrs Henderson's steel railings to make a melody. It was like playing a big rusty xylophone. The faster I ran, the higher the notes sounded out. But there was no such joy on Friday nights. As darkness fell on the last day of the week, my mood would grow grave. For Friday night was when robbers came up from down the Shankill for easy pickings.

The papers themselves were heavier too on a Friday, because of the job advertisement section – but not much heavier, because there weren't that many jobs. I sometimes looked through the employment pages to see what I might do when I graduated from newspaper delivery, but there was never anything. Then I noticed that there were always more death notices than job advertisements in the *Belfast Telegraph*, so I came to the comforting conclusion that by the time I was eighteen years old, enough people would have died for me to get one of their jobs.

There were undoubtedly pros and cons to collecting the paper money. At the caravan site in Millisle we went to every summer, I met paperboys who delivered in East Belfast, where they built the *Titanic* that sank. They didn't collect the money because their Oul' Mac didn't trust them. At least our Oul' Mac gave us the chance not to thieve! As a Shankill paperboy, I didn't often get the chance to feel morally superior, but it felt good to be able to claim the moral high ground over East Belfast boys, because they seemed to think they were so much more Protestant than us. Apparently, East Belfast customers had to go to the shop to pay their paper money on the way home from the shipyard. The result of this was that the paperboys there only got one tip a year, at Christmas. This was the downside of having no financial responsibilities. No money, no robbers – but then again no money, no tips. Collecting the paper money every Friday night opened up the possibility of year-round tipping, so I soon decided that the benefits of regular tips outweighed the risks of being robbed.

Everyone loved Friday nights, as a rule. There was a lightness in the air, like on Christmas Eve and the Eleventh Night. Friday was the night you had no hateful homework. It was the night when Dad came home from the foundry, paid and happy, and he gave us boys 50p and Mum a Walnut Whip. (When he got overtime, we got a pound note each and she got a box of Milk Tray.) Friday was the night of *Crackerjack* at five minutes to five on BBC 1. Everyone in my street loved it, but I had to miss it. While all the other kids of my age were glued to the screen, trying to win a *Crackerjack* pencil – which was nearly as good as winning a *Blue Peter* badge — I was out in the dark, running the gauntlet of doing papers and collecting money. I was learning to make sacrifices for my career.

Growing up in the Upper Shankill, you soon learned that you were better than the people in the Lower Shankill. It was good to be better than someone somewhere. Any trouble or crime was usually blamed on 'that dirt down the Road'. The houses were older and smaller down the Shankill — two up and two down, if you were lucky. Everyone down there was on the dole and smoked and nobody did the Eleven Plus.

We, on the other hand, lived in the Shankill's only privately owned housing estate. So we were special. One lady on my paper round, who got a *People's Friend*, always corrected you if you called it an 'estate'. She preferred you to say a 'private development'. We had front and back gardens in our estate, and not everyone put a flag out for the Twelfth. Our house had a phone, some of the neighbours owned shops on the Road, two of my customers had new Ford Cortinas, and a man in the next street was even a teacher.

Mrs Grant from No. 2 actually had a son at university. He had passed his Eleven Plus and gone to 'Methody' on the Malone Road. Mrs Grant said it was better than Belfast Royal Academy because there were no Catholics living anywhere nearby. Her son was a genius, and so he had gone to university in England. It was very important to her that everyone should know about Samuel's academic achievements. If you ever found yourself in the queue behind Mrs Grant in the Post Office when your mother was collecting the family allowance or sending a postal order to the Great Universal Club Book, you would hear Mrs Grant ending every conversation with a noticeable increase in volume, and always with the same words: 'Our Samuel's still at university in England, you know.' The whole queue would roll its eyes.

I never, ever saw Samuel. He was always at university in England, it seemed. Maybe he is still there. He was like Charlie in *Charlie's Angels*. You heard a lot about him and all of his heroic achievements, but you never actually saw his face. Samuel didn't seem to come home much, even though Mrs Grant talked such a lot about him, and her husband, Richard, was awful bad with his chest and throat and everything.

The kids in the council estate on the other side of the road called our warren of red-brick semis 'Snob Hill'. They were jealous because we were so rich. Some of their rows of red-brick terrace houses were boarded up and we called them 'smelly'. Of course, we were jealous of them too. They had shops and a green for their bonfire, a flute band and a community centre for paramilitaries, and the black taxis stopped right at the entrance to their estate. All we had was a telephone box, a post box and neat gardens.

Every year, one or two children from our estate, like me, passed the Eleven Plus and went to grammar school. We weren't really supposed to. But regardless of this fact, my parents made education a priority, to the astonishing extent that passing the Eleven Plus was more important than not having a United Ireland. 'No son of mine is going to end up in a filthy foundry like me,' was my father's refrain.

If doing the Eleven Plus meant that I was a snob, passing the Eleven Plus meant that I was a super snob. And going to a grammar school meant that I was Prince Charles. Yet, on my first day at Belfast Royal Academy, I would learn that I was much less of a snob than I could ever have imagined. There were not too many paperboys from the Shankill around. Not too many Shankill boys around at all, in fact. I had been an impressive angelfish in a small goldfish bowl at Springhill Primary School, but at Belfast Royal Academy I was a guppy with raggedy fins in the huge expanse of Lough Neagh. Wee hard men from the Lower Shankill delighted in reducing the Belfast Royal Academy to a breast-related acronym: 'Have you been inside a BRA all day, ya big fruit?!' they would shout.

It was at grammar school that I first discovered that most people made no distinction between Lower Shankill and Upper Shankill. We were all dirt.

The robbers from the Lower Shankill weren't big-time hoods or paramilitaries. They weren't like those Great Train Robbers or Jesse James on TV. Neither were they wee fat men in masks with black-and-white striped shirts and swag bags, like in *The Beano*. They were just wee hard men a few years older than me. I got stopped by them all the time. I guess I must have looked soft in my blue duffle coat and grammar-school scarf.

But, in spite of appearances, I was hard to rob. I didn't fight. I couldn't fight. Sure there were enough people in Belfast fighting anyway. So I just used my head instead. I kept an eye out for suspicious-looking teenage males in my streets on my patch on Friday nights. They were easy to identify. They walked like wee hard men, half march and half swagger. They wore tartan scarves and white parallel trousers and smoked.

Once I spied a suspected hood, I could disappear into the darkness through holes in familiar fences, under camouflage of garden hedges. Then, just in case my attempts at invisibility should fail, I hid the paper notes down my socks and dropped the coins down my boots. Robbers hadn't the brains to suspect that my Doc Martens held a cash stash. They thought boots were just for kicking your head in. So, when they ordered me to empty my pockets, or else they would 'smash my f**kin' face in', and when they searched my pockets for cash, they got nothing. You should have heard the victory jangle of coins in my boots as I leapt over prim Protestant hedges between semis after an attempted robbery. There was, however, a cost to my zealous protection of Oul' Mac's profits – painful blisters on my feet, from running on grinding ten- and fifty-pence pieces.

The worst part of being a Shankill paperboy was the constant fear that the robbers out there in the darkness would employ more violent techniques. It worried my parents too. I was under strict instructions from my father that I should inform him of any encounters with suspected robbers. I rarely did. I had worked out how to handle them myself. I used my head, like the Doctor preventing an invasion of Daleks. Instead of hand-to-hand combat, I too attempted to come up with a clever and cunning plan.

But one Friday night, it was different. The wee hood

was only about sixteen, but he scared me. He wouldn't give up. I had already done my disappearing act a couple of times. He had already stopped me once, used the obligatory 'kick your f**kin' head in' threat, and made me empty my pockets. Of course the money was safely snuggled between my toes, but he took my chewing gum and my *Thunderbird 2* badge. Even that didn't seem to satisfy him, however. He kept hanging around and following me and I had to stop collecting money altogether.

The wee hood in question wasn't much taller than me, but he was plumper, and his parallels and Doc Martens were worn. He wore his trouser legs higher up the shin than me. This was an important indicator of the level of potential threat. For girls, the higher the parallels, the bigger the millie. A 'millie' was a girl that smoked, said 'f**k' a lot and wound her chewing gum around her fingers between chews. A millie was the opposite of Sharon Burgess. They could be good craic, but you wouldn't want to kiss one. With boys, the higher your parallels, the harder you were. My big brother's parallels were always higher than mine. Of course, you had to be very careful. If your trouser legs went above your knees, then they just became shorts and that meant you were a fruit.

The wee hood's hair looked like his ma had cut it. He looked like he couldn't afford to get it feathered in His n' Hers beside the graveyard. He was spottier than anyone in my class in school. He had even more spots than Frankie Jones in French who played the drums, liked heavy-metal music and hid dirty magazines in his schoolbag.

My assailant had a bizarre speech impediment. In all of his brief communications with me, he started every sentence with the word 'f\*\*kin''. It was supposed to sound hard, but it just sounded peculiar:

'F\*\*kin' wee lad, have you any money on ye?'

'F\*\*kin' you there, who do you think yer looking at?'

'F\*\*kin' when do you collect the f\*\*kin' money here?'

He was seriously interfering with the execution of my professional duties. So I slipped through a hole in the Coopers' fence. All the Coopers had blonde hair and a turn in their eye, but their granda was brilliant at bowls and they got the *Weekly News* and a *TV Times*. I jumped over a few red-brick walls, landing uncomfortably on a bootful of loose change, and eventually arrived at my own back door.

'Dad, there's a robber!' I said breathlessly as I burst into the house, kicking off my boots and launching a fleet of coins across the sitting-room shag pile. My father had just changed out of his dirty blue foundry overalls into his new beige trousers from the Club Book.

'Right!' he barked angrily. 'Where is the wee bastard? Show me!'

I knew he meant business when he stubbed out his cigar in the seashell ashtray from Millisle. He had given up chain-smoking cigarettes because they gave you cancer. Now he chain-smoked Hamlet cigars instead. The living room was just as smoky, but I preferred the smell. Daddy particularly enjoyed smoking a Hamlet cigar, while sipping a black coffee and sucking cherry menthol Tunes as he watched a documentary on BBC 2. 'Your father's a very clever man,' my mother would say. I think she was referring to the documentaries.

Dad went upstairs straight away and took out the large wooden pickaxe handle from under his bed. This had appeared under my parents' bed when the Troubles started. I think it was meant to be our family's protection against a rumoured IRA invasion of our estate. The Provos seemed somewhat better equipped, so I had worked out an escape plan to hide in the roof space when they attacked. I had devised the exact same plan should there ever be a Dalek invasion, because I knew they wouldn't be able to use the stepladders.

Within seconds, we were in our red Ford Escort respray on the trail of the wee hood. I was now more shaken by the commissioning of the pickaxe handle than by the robber. I didn't regard my father as a violent man. Yes, he gave me a few hidings with the strap for my cheek, but he wasn't a fighter and he scorned the paramilitaries. 'No son of mine will be getting involved with any of those paramilitary gabshites!' he would pronounce regularly.

We drove around the estate a few times, searching for the robber. I got a surge of excitement with the realisation that the predator in parallels had now become the prey. My father would grab the wee hood, bring him back to our house and phone the police. The police would bring him home to his wee two-up, two-down. His Da would give him a good hiding and he would never attempt to rob a paperboy again.

But what happened next shocked me. I spotted the robber at the top of another paperboy's street. I pointed him out. My father abruptly stopped the car, pulling up the handbrake with a screech.

'You stay here!' he commanded, as he grabbed the pickaxe handle from the back seat and sprang out of the car. He ran up behind the wee hood in the dark. It was raining now, and everything looked blurred through the windscreen. I watched my father unleash the weapon with force across the wee lad's back. I feared he was going to kill him.

The hood stumbled on the impact, yelped like a beaten dog and ran for his life. Now I felt sorry for him. All this for a packet of Wrigley's and a *Thunderbird 2* badge. Dad had hit him so hard that he had lost his own balance and landed in a puddle on the pavement in his good trousers and cut his hand on the kerb. He looked like Captain James T. Kirk, after fighting a monster alone on a dangerous alien planet, all sweaty and bloody, determined to save the crew of the USS *Enterprise*. By this stage, however, I just wanted him beamed up as quickly as possible.

'That's the end of him!' my father announced when he returned to the car, soaked, breathless, bleeding and sweating.

'It nearly was!' I thought. 'No son of mine is gettin' robbed by no wee hood!' Dad proclaimed.

I had expected the robber to be brought to the police: now I was afraid the police would arrest my father. Fortunately, the RUC had other priorities at the time.

My father drove us home very quickly, and his heavy breath steamed up the inside of the windscreen. This was the same car we went on picnics in. Within a few minutes we were back home and he was just Dad again, falling off the sofa, laughing at posh Englishmen talking to a dead parrot on *Monty Python's Flying Circus*.

My mother was appalled by the state of his soaked and shredded slacks. She had fifteen more weeks at 99p to pay for them, and now they were ruined. She ended up using them to clean the windows. But I knew she was secretly pleased by the protective pickaxe blows for her son. She tended to Dad's injured hand like Florence Nightingale nursing the soldiers in my school history book. She called him 'Eric, love' and he called her 'Betty, love.'

Everything was all right again. I felt safe and protected by the strength and toughness of this new action-hero dad. He was like Clint Eastwood, only bald with glasses, and this Wild West was in Belfast.

I understood that this was the Northern Ireland way. If someone hits you, you hit him back harder. It felt satisfying and powerful, but I knew this way solved absolutely nothing. I saw it every day in Belfast. Tit-for-tat for tit-for-tat. An eye for an eye, a tooth for a tooth, a Catholic for a Protestant. Men excusing heinous acts of inhumanity to protect or liberate 'their' people, belligerently sowing pain and bitterness for generations to come. I suppose it made them feel potent and powerful too. I got a little taste of it that night with my father and the wee hood, but I spat it out. It sickened me. There had to be another way. I resolved that I would be Belfast's first pacifist paperboy.

# CHAPTER THREE

## *the belfast crack*

'Patience is a virtue,' said Mrs Rowing, in a gently reproachful manner.

The Rowings lived just around the corner from us, in the newest red-brick semis in our estate. These newer houses were basically the same as ours, but being more modern, they had no larders, smaller gardens, and the toilet and bath were in the same room. All the modernity of 1970s Shankill living was reflected in these most up-to-date of dwellings, which had central heating in some rooms and an outside water tap at the back door. The outside tap seemed to impress everyone, which I couldn't really understand, because my granny had a toilet outside her back door and it impressed no one. Running water in your back yard was not a universally applauded amenity.

Our family home however, while it was one of the older semis, was years ahead even of the newer residences. My father had used his fitter's skills and had already installed central heating in our house all by himself with pipes he had borrowed from the foundry. I had held the torch for him in the dark under the floorboards, as he hammered stubborn pipes into shape to keep his family warm. I was in awe of my Da's skill and heroism. I noticed that even when he sweated big drops, he kept on working. As I held the increasingly heavy industrial torch — which my Da had also borrowed from the foundry — I distracted myself from the ache in my arm with thoughts of how people in Belfast had hidden from German bombers under floorboards just like this during the Blitz, when my father was a wee boy — not that long ago, really. At night sometimes, I had bad dreams of screaming air-raid sirens and German bombers, like in black-and-white movies, droning in the distance and then appearing in the skies above the Black Mountain to drop hundreds of bombs in our direction — one of which could be heading for your house, for all you knew. When people on the Shankill talked about the Blitz, they always mentioned Percy Street, where a bomb had landed on the air-raid shelter and killed whole families. It sounded even worse than the Troubles to me.

Looking at Mrs Rowing as she held the door open for me, I was thinking that I had never heard anyone say 'patience is a virtue' before, except for *Robinson Crusoe* on BBC 1 on a Saturday morning, as he walked around and around his island surrounded by black-and-white waves.

The other neighbours up our way didn't talk like that. I would have been more used to something like: 'Houl your horses, ya cheeky wee skitter!' This was the Upper Shankill, after all. Certainly more upmarket than Lower Shankill, I was always told, but hardly Malone or Cultra, where the posh accents lived. But the Rowings were gentle and well-spoken Church of Ireland people. Mrs Rowing said her 'ings', collected for cancer and got a knitting magazine. In spite of their unusual name, I certainly couldn't imagine these lovely people ever actually having a row with anyone!

Mr Rowing was my long-suffering guitar teacher, and on the night in question, I was early for my Friday evening lesson. Guitar lessons had followed a similar pattern to the advent of my paperboy career. My big brother had started first, and I simply had to follow. Then, as soon as I began, he retired. The fact that I had become old enough to engage in any activity seemed to immediately deem it inappropriate for him. This precedent would, however, later be broken when it came to drinking Harp and going to the bookies.

It was windy and cold that night as the red-brick semis of the Upper Shankill clung to the side of the Black Mountain. I had to push the Rowings' doorbell three times instead of giving it the usual solitary ring. My fingers were still numb from folding forty-eight *Belfast Telegraphs* in the freezing rain, followed by a furious scrubbing to cleanse them from black ink so as to have dirt-free fingers for my guitar lesson. With my fresh and freezing fingers now plunged into my temperate duffle-coat pockets, I stamped from foot to foot in anticipation of the warmth of the Rowings' well-kept semi. I had just finished my Friday-night paper round and safely collected the paper money for the week from all of my customers. There had been no attempted robberies by wee hoods this week: the inclement weather seemed to be more of a hindrance to their profession than it was to mine. On a cold wet Friday night with bombs in the pubs, most people stayed in. Very few of my clientele had pretended not to be in to evade my monetary demands, and so I had a warm and welcome bootful of profits.

To tell the truth, I was a little offended at the 'patience is a virtue' remark. It was clearly a gentle rebuke. Mrs Rowing was normally encouragingly cheerful, and my mother always said she was a lady. I was sure that patience was indeed a virtue, but I was in a hurry: it was freezing cold. Music was the fruit of my paperboy labours: from my £1.50 wages, I paid for strings, plectrums and music books, as well as 20p for this regular guitar lesson. I was keen to get out of the cold and get started. I wanted to play like Paul McCartney, so I had a lot of catching up to do.

Every week, Mrs Rowing would welcome me with a pleasant smile and usher me in to wait my turn in her well-ordered living room, complete with a cornered television. The decor was old-fashioned compared to our living room, as the Rowings weren't as young and 'with it' as my parents. For a start, they wore slacks instead of flares. An ancient wind-up wooden clock ticked relentlessly on the mantelpiece and chimed every fifteen minutes: it must have been a hundred years old. The Rowings had old dark wooden furniture that reminded me of the tables and chairs that came out of my other granny's house after my other granda died, when the Protestants were moving out of the Springfield Road. We on the other hand had the latest lava lamp on hire purchase from Gillespie & Wilson. The Rowings had delph ornaments of cocker spaniels and a copper coal bucket on the hearth; we had woodchip wallpaper and venetian blinds. They had a traditional patterned rug; we had verdant shag pile. The only old thing in our house was a bookcase my mother had bought when her numbers came up on the Premium Bonds, before I was born. It was called a 'libranza', and it already looked much too dated for my modern eyes.

Mr Rowing gave the guitar lessons in their sitting room. It was obviously the 'good' room, with a china cabinet and white lace doilies on the arms of the chairs and sofa. Opposite the sitting room was the kitchen, where Mrs Rowing lived. Although there was always a smell of freshly baked scones coming from the kitchen, I never once saw a single scone on a Friday night. Mrs Rowing was always baking, and yet there was only the two of them in the house, so I wondered who ate all the scones. I never actually got to see into Mrs Rowing's working kitchen either, but I imagined that it contained a high fruit-scone tower piled up in the middle of her lino.

Inside the antique china cabinet in the sitting room where the lessons took place, a pair of tiny white lace baby boots rested on a well-polished glass shelf. Old and faded like Miss Havisham's wedding dress in *Great Expectations* in English class, these tiny curiosities would catch my eye every week, and I wondered who the baby might have been. Maybe they had belonged to Mr Rowing when he was a wee baby, with tiny hands of less than the span of a fret. Perhaps they were Mrs Rowing's, from a time long before her first fruit scone. Or maybe they belonged to the couple's mysterious long-lost son, who had fled Belfast to escape from the Church of Ireland and the Troubles, to play gypsy guitar in a travelling circus in Czechoslovakia behind the Iron Curtain, where the nuclear bombs were pointing right at us.

Mr Rowing was an accomplished guitarist. On the walls of the sitting room hung faded, framed black-and-white photographs of him playing old-fashioned guitars in showbands in the fifties. Everyone's parents had met at the dance halls in Belfast in the fifties where the showbands played. My mother and father had met at The Ritz, and I was sure Mr Rowing must have performed there. I wanted to believe that Mr Rowing had played guitar during their first dance, when a young fitter called Eric from the Springfield Road had asked an innocent seamstress called Betty from the Donegall Road for a jive. My parents had loved the showbands. When the Miami Showband were shot, my mother cried at every news bulletin and my father's silence scared me. It was like the Troubles had taken over for them, and all the old happy times were gone for ever.

Mr Rowing looked like a young Bill Haley. He still had dark, teddy-boy hair, and he was the only customer in the whole estate who got *Guitar Player* magazine. Unlike me, he had big thick fingers, like sausage rolls from the Ormo Mini Shop. I assumed that playing guitar for all these years had made his fingers grow, and these sizeable and dexterous digits were perfect for switching and sustaining complicated chords. I hoped that one day my hands would become as strong and tough, so that no malevolent metal string would ever slice into them again.

A big gentle man, Mr Rowing was always encouraging and always friendly. Most men his age shouted a lot, but he never once got annoyed at my limited musical progress, tolerating my lack of practice between lessons and praising me for infinitesimal improvements. Mr Rowing seemed to understand the virtue of patience. Maybe Mrs Rowing had taught him.

The first tune I learned with Mr Rowing was, 'Hang Down Your Head, Tom Dooley'. It was ancient, and country and western, and more than a bit depressing to my young ears, but it only required the ability to play two chords. The doleful lyric went as follows:

> Hang down your head, Tom Dooley,
> Hang down your head and cry,
> Hang down your head, Tom Dooley,
> Poor boy, you're bound to die.

I played that song until my fingers stopped stinging, my family's ears stopped smarting and my performance had become flawless. Tom Dooley died a thousand times in my bedroom, but I knew that once I had mastered this piece, Mr Rowing would, as he had promised, teach me something from the Hit Parade. I couldn't wait. Would it be something from *Top of the Pops*, like 'Maggie May' by Rod Stewart?

But no. My next piece would be 'Apache' by The Shadows: an old hit from the sixties by a group with glasses that my Granny liked because 'that lovely wee good livin' boy, Cliff Richard, used to sing with them, so he did'. Just like Tom Dooley, I hung down my head and cried.

With every new chord I mastered, I anticipated learning a brand-new song, something groovy from the seventies. I knew I could never handle the intricacy of 'Bohemian Rhapsody' by Queen in three chords, but could Mr Rowing not at least accommodate my rock-star longings by teaching me 'Mull of Kintyre'? In the end, I took matters into my own hands, spending all my paperboy tips one Saturday morning on the sheet music by Paul McCartney. It was half-price in the smoke-damage sale in Crymble's music shop beside the City Hall. The Provos had tried to burn Crymble's down, and so I feared there would be no music shops allowed in a United Ireland.

Once I had the sheet music in front of me, I taught myself 'Mull of Kintyre'. Mr Rowing had been teaching me the basics, but now I was emerging as an artist in my own right, like Michael Jackson leaving the Jackson Five. As I played Paul McCartney's inspiring anthem in my bedroom, I imagined I was performing it in my duffle-coat, out on a windswept Scottish hillside on the Mull of Kintyre itself, which was across the sea from Barry's Amusements in Portrush. Earnestly poring over every chord and with every word I sang, I could see Sharon Burgess standing beside me, her hair blowing in the Celtic winds while she gazed up at me, admiring my strums, just like Linda McCartney with Paul.

Mr Rowing also promised me new songs at Christmas. I yearned to learn 'Merry Christmas Everybody' by Slade, but he taught me 'Silent Night' and 'Away in a Manger'. Although my guitar-playing skills progressed and my ambition was limitless, sadly my repertoire never really escaped from the 1960s.

Pamela Burnside was always in just before me on a Friday night. Pamela's parents were big fans of country and western. They had a signed photo of 'Big T' from Downtown Radio on their mantelpiece. Mr Burnside had a Kenny Rogers beard and a snake belt, and he sold second-hand cars down the Road. My mother said he was a real cowboy. Pamela's mum had the longest hair on the Shankill – like Crystal Gayle – and she sang 'Amazing Grace' in an American accent and wore cowboy boots at the Annual Beetle Drive for Biafran babies in the church hall. The Burnsides and their small white poodle wore Union Jack stetsons on the Twelfth of July, and they wanted their daughter Pamela to be Tammy Wynette. They made her wear a suede country-and-western jacket with a fringe on the arms that got caught in the spokes of her bike. I'm fairly certain she would have preferred a Bay City Rollers T-shirt like everybody else. Anyway, she just didn't have the kind of talent needed to be the next Tammy Wynette.

Every Friday night, as I waited my turn in Mrs Rowing's living room, I could just about make out from the next room the muffled sound of Pamela's desperate attempts at 'Hang Down Your Head, Tom Dooley'. She rarely got the one chord change right, and I would hear Mr Rowing saying kindly, 'Yes, that's getting better now' — although it clearly wasn't.

Tom Dooley must have died a million times in Mr Rowing's sitting room on those Friday nights. Poor Pamela always emerged from her lesson red-faced and fearful. I could tell that she felt ashamed of her poor performance and knew rightly that she was dreading the inevitable inquiry into her progress with the plectrum which awaited her at home. Pamela still couldn't manage 'Tom Dooley', yet she knew only too well that her doggedly optimistic parents were already expecting her to deliver  the musical complexities of 'D-I-V-O-R-C-E'.

As I waited in the living room for my lesson, thinking up excuses for not having practised enough during the week just past, I would watch *It's a Knockout* on the 1960s black-and-white push-button television. I usually longed for

Pammy Wynette's lesson to overrun so that I would get to watch an extra five minutes of *Jeux Sans Frontières*, as the French called it. But Mr Rowing was always merciful enough to Pamela to ensure that the lesson was not drawn out any longer than necessary.

*Jeux Sans Frontières* was like the *Eurovision Song Contest* without the songs. It was live by satellite from a football pitch in Belgium. I was astounded at how they beamed the pictures from Europe to Belfast via outer space. It was like when a Klingon from an enemy ship on the other side of a space anomaly was able to speak to Captain Kirk on the big screen on the bridge of the USS *Enterprise*. I was fascinated by the sound of Continental cheers, the whistles and horns and the spectacle of Germans, French and Italians and others in comical costumes, falling over each other as they fought for victory in Europe. I thought it odd that thirty years earlier these nations had been slaughtering one another. My granny still wasn't too keen on Germans. Any mention of Germany evoked a tirade of abuse about 'that oul' brute, Hitler!' According to her, he was worse than Gerry Adams. Now these former enemies were having ridiculous races in giant clown costumes to the tinny satellite echoes of hysterical laughter from Stuart Hall, the jovial presenter – and all in the name of light-entertainment television. 'Patience is a virtue', I thought.

I had a small Spanish guitar. It had been my first really grown-up Christmas present – that is, not from Santa. It had cost twenty weeks at 99p from the Club Book. Okay, it wasn't a red star-shaped electric guitar like on

*Top of the Pops*, and I couldn't imagine Marc Bolan playing it — but I loved my guitar. It was in many ways like my first girlfriend, Sharon Burgess: it never felt cold when I embraced it or rested my chin on its shoulder.

My guitar was a honeyed yellow colour, with a simple dotted line design around the edges. It retained a lovely smell of wood and fresh varnish. At first, the strings made painful impressions on the fingers of my right hand. I was left-handed — like Paul McCartney — but we couldn't afford an expensive left-handed guitar, so I got a right-handed one, restrung the other way round. Hence I always appeared to be playing my guitar upside down, with my plectrum guard above, rather than below, the blows of my energetic strumming. My big regrets were that I was neither Paul McCartney, nor right-handed, nor rich.

Eventually, just as the Germans were playing their Joker Card to win extra points in a raft race in gorilla suits, my absorption was interrupted by the sound of Pammy Wynette being gently escorted from the premises by an exhausted-looking Mr Rowing. Pammy generally ignored me, ever since we had fallen out at the bonfire one year, when I had said that country and western was for oul' lads and oul' dolls. But on this evening, as she said her apologies and goodbyes to Mr Rowing, she turned back towards me with vital information.

'It said on Radio Luxembourg last night that the Bay City Rollers is comin' to Belfast,' she pronounced, with the look of superiority that could only come from being the bearer of such exclusive, fresh and earth-shattering information.

'Brilliant!' I exclaimed. 'Are yousens goin'?'

'Aye,' Pamela responded. 'Are yousens?"

'Aye,' I replied excitedly.

The word 'yousens' in this context referred to oneself and all of one's friends. It was clear that most of the teenage population of the Upper Shankill would be going to this great event. Tickets would be like gold dust, and tartan material would be at a premium.

As I entered Mrs Rowing's good room for my lesson, I dreamed of playing guitar on stage with the Rollers. It seemed promising when Mr Rowing said that he would begin to teach me a new, 'more up-to-date' number. Yet I was once again disappointed: it was 'Love Me Tender' by the pre-fat Elvis! Yet again, an old-fashioned song from the sixties that only old people liked and that most people would soon forget, instead of a modern classic, like 'Shang-a-Lang'. However, I got my Cs and Fs and Ds in the right order, and Mr Rowing appreciated my talent so much that I got an extra fifteen minutes. I was his last student of the night, because I had to finish collecting the paper money and avoid hoods and robbers on a Friday night – and so no one was ever waiting through the final minutes of *It's a Knockout* for me to finish. As a result of this fact, and Mr Rowing's good nature and genuine enthusiasm, I often got an extra fifteen minutes for my 20 pence.

After my extended guitar lesson at the Rowings' that windy winter night, I ran the short distance home through the spitting rain, with the tune of 'Love Me Tender' repeating itself irritatingly in my head. I sped past Titch McCracken, who was desperately trying to light a sly cigarette in the wind behind Mrs Patterson's hydrangea. Overhead droned a noisy British Army helicopter, keeping an eye on West Belfast.

Before the Troubles, I had never seen a real helicopter, apart from the one that *Skippy the Bush Kangaroo* on UTV would alert to save a boy who had fallen down an abandoned mine shaft in Australia. But now helicopters were an ever-present whirr, looking down on us, their searchlights shining on targeted streets to illuminate any wrongdoing. This heavenly Super Trouper was in fact one of the more enjoyable experiences of 1970s Belfast – at least for me, and other boys like me. The boom of bombs pummelled the marrow in my growing bones. The deadly staccato sound of gunfire ripped at my tender heart. But the night-time sight of a helicopter searchlight rushing up your street until you were standing in quasi-daylight was as exhilarating as the rollercoaster at Barry's on the Sunday school excursion to Bangor! It was the most exciting thing to go up our street apart from the poke man, the UDA and the Ormo Mini Shop.

On the fateful night in question, coming home from my guitar lesson, I looked up to see the searchlight flicker across the disrespectful blue-black sky. Reaching the rickety front gate of our house, I halted as the light leapt up the street towards me and all at once I was illuminated in its full, stark glare. The rays reflected off the rusty gate I had tried to paint over for 30p for the scouts during Bob-a-Job Week.

'I hope they don't think my Spanish guitar is a machine gun from up there!' I suddenly thought. For a moment, I imagined a new boy having to take over my paper round the next day, delivering *Belfast Telegraphs* with the headline: '12-year-old Terrorist with Suspicious Instrument Shot Dead'. We weren't allowed toy guns or fireworks in case they got us shot, but I had never before considered that carrying a Spanish guitar could transform me into a legitimate target. Blinded by the light and distracted by all of this catastrophising, I was unprepared for the impact.

The malicious wind blew the steel gate into my defenceless wee guitar. I heard the crack; I knew it was serious. The guitar was covered by a soft, blue pretend leather case that my aunt had bought me for my birthday. (The hard guitar cases used by professionals were too dear to be sold in the Club Book, even over sixty weeks.) This soft blue case kept the rain off my Spanish guitar, but it lacked the rigidity required to protect the vulnerable instrument from damage. I couldn't see inside just yet, but I knew already that my precious guitar had been seriously wounded.

When I finally got indoors and saw a big crack in my guitar which ran from head to bridge, I cried. Of course, my father did his 'fix-it' best with glue he had borrowed from the foundry, but I had to come to terms with the fact that my guitar was permanently fractured. There was nothing I could do: it would always be split. Sadly, just like Belfast would be all my life. I yearned for things to be different, but I couldn't envisage it any other way.

From that night on, there was a new melancholy in my rendition of 'Hang Down Your Head, Tom Dooley'. Yet somewhere in my mind I still held on to thoughts of *Jeux*

*Sans Frontières* and Europe and hope. And I remembered that patience is a virtue.

# CHAPTER FOUR

## *secrets in school*

Being a paperboy had to be a secret once I started Belfast Royal Academy, as I soon learned. Living up the Shankill, having a Ford Escort respray and a father who worked in a foundry near the Falls Road were just a few of the other facts best kept hidden. No one ever said it out loud, but I picked up the cues from the dominant rugger boys that this information was best kept discreetly folded away – like the *Woman's Own* you kept at the bottom of your paperbag for the middle-aged man with dyed hair who still lived with his mammy in No. 91.

I thought I had more secrets to keep than James Bond, until I got to know Thomas O'Hara, another wee boy in my class with something to hide. I had never met any 'O'' anythings before. It was whispered in the playground that wee Thomas with the curly hair and freckles was, in fact, a real Catholic. This was confirmed when someone overheard him saying 'Haitch Blocks' instead of 'H Blocks'. And David Pritchard, who didn't believe in God and rebelliously refused to close his eyes during prayers in Assembly, had spotted Thomas crossing himself at the 'Amens'. David, evidently a Protestant atheist, was appalled and told everybody.

Wee Thomas was the first Catholic I had ever spoken to, although I had once sung along with Val Doonican's rendition of 'Paddy McGinty's Goat' from his rocking chair on BBC 1 on a Saturday night after *Doctor Who*. At eleven years old, I was very young to be meeting one of 'the other sort' for the first time. Most people in Belfast left it until they were at least eighteen, or preferably never did it at all. Titch McCracken said you could tell someone was a Catholic if their eyes were too close together, but I wasn't convinced, because one of the other paperboys, Billy Cooper, was practically cross-eyed, but he played a flute in The Loyal Sons of Ulster Band. And you couldn't get more Protestant than that.

I would get the biggest shock I had had since John Noakes announced he was leaving *Blue Peter* when remarkably — against all the odds and contrary to all that I had heard from both heaven and earth — I realised that wee Thomas O'Hara was in fact dead-on. Before this, my primary experience of Catholics had been limited to cross men on *Scene Around Six* who made my father shout. Of course, Dad also yelled when the Reverend Ian Paisley came on the news, which was baffling because Big Ian was the opposite of a Catholic. And while my granny said Paisley was 'our saviour', my father called him 'Bucket Mouth'. All the other paperboys said, like Granny, that without Big Ian we would be 'sold down the river', but I could never work out where the river was. Maybe it was in Ballymena.

I made friends with wee Thomas on my first day at grammar school. Out of all the boys and girls in my class, he was the only one who wasn't wearing a brand-new school uniform in the first week. He told me he was getting his blazer at the weekend, but when I told my mother, she said, 'God love that poor wee Catholic boy; they can't even afford to buy the crater a uniform!' This seemed to clash with the proud assertion I had often heard, that 'we're just as poor as them, you know.'

In fact, Thomas proved what I had always suspected, but would never have dared to articulate to either my paperboy peers or my Sunday school teacher: that Catholics were just the same as us! I couldn't understand why such an astounding discovery had never made the front page of any of the *Belfast Telegraphs* I delivered.

Wee Thomas was one of the few people in my class who would have made a good paperboy, and he was certainly much more like me than any of the rugger boys. They made clever jokes in the rugby changing rooms about sheep and masturbation, but they never dropped a single 'ing'. The rugger boys at school were the first people I ever heard putting a complete 'ing' onto the end of 'f**k', and it just didn't work. They thought they were dead hard, eff-ing and blind-ing, but I thought they sounded ridiculous because I knew what real effin' and blindin' was. They were in their element kicking each other in a scrum, but I wondered how they would deal with hoods and robbers on a Friday night up the Shankill.

The only difference between Thomas and me was that he didn't make a secret of who he was or where he lived. Unlike me, he didn't seem to feel the need to keep secrets at school. Maybe my shame at not being prosperous was pure Presbyterian. Once wee Thomas and I became friends, I even learned that he was from Ardoyne, where the IRA lived. Of course, I never asked him if he wanted a United Ireland, worshipped Mary and supported the IRA. I just assumed he must be one of the 'good ones' who didn't do all that.

However, one thing that I knew for sure was that wee Thomas and I shared an aspiration for something far more important than fighting between Catholics and Protestants. We were both willing to set aside all ancient rivalries for the sake of a common purpose – to dominate the pop-music charts. Along with two other school friends, me and wee Thomas decided to start a rock band. The other members of the band were Ian, who got the *New Musical Express* and sang in an English accent, and Stephen, who played a tambourine like David Cassidy. We wanted to be Status Quo, but we had limited talent and resources. All we had was my split Spanish guitar and an old bodhrán from Thomas's granda's shed. I never told my granny that I was in a band with an Irish drum, as I assumed this might be dangerous territory.

Although we tried very hard, we could never make 'Hang Down Your Head, Tom Dooley' sound like Status Quo. We decided to copy ABBA by using the first letter of each of our names to spell out the name of the band. We would be just like Agnetha, Björn, Benny and Anni-Frid. However, this idea proved problematic when we realised we had Thomas on drums, a lead vocalist called Ian, Tony on lead guitar and a tambourine player called Stephen . . .

The TITS were doomed. We split up during rehearsal one day, before playing even one gig at the scout hut, when I mistakenly expressed an interest in the forthcoming Bay City Rollers concert in the Ulster Hall. Ever since Pammy Wynette had told me the Rollers were coming to Belfast, I had been scouring the *Belfast Telegraph* announcements pages every night for news of dates and prices. My customers were even beginning to notice that I was ten minutes late every night. When, at band practice at Ian's house one day, I casually mentioned that I was engaging in this research, the revelation exposed deep and unexpected artistic differences within the TITS. Ian was very angry. He said he was too serious about rock and roll to be in a band with a guitarist who wanted to see 'them bloody teenybopper sell-outs' in concert.

I didn't know what a 'teenybopper sell-out' was, because I didn't read the *New Musical Express*, but Ian seemed to take it to heart. I was just innocently hoping that the Rollers concert wouldn't be sold out before I could get a ticket, but Ian said members of the TITS should only go to see serious rock bands, like Status Quo. He accused the Bay City Rollers of not being able to play their own instruments. I thought this was ironic, because we had been experiencing exactly the same difficulties ourselves. Ian sneered that the Scottish superstars should be called the 'Gay Shitty Fakers', and finally announced with an arrogant flourish that he no longer wanted to be one of the TITS. He threw down the handle of his little sister's skipping rope, which he had been using as an improvised microphone, and walked out of the band practice, slamming the door behind him. (The dramatic effect was spoiled slightly when he had to come back in again because we were in his sitting room and his mammy had wheeled in a hostess trolley with cups of tea she had made for us and an apple tart.)

Ian's walkout left the band without a lead vocalist, and without a vowel. Stephen would soon follow. He said he wanted to concentrate on disco dancing and that he had never been that interested in the TITS anyway. Thomas and I realised that we couldn't go on as a duo, even though we knew it was working well for Donny and Marie Osmond, and so we decided to concentrate on solo projects.

The teachers at BRA occasionally provided us with a clear insight into our place in the world. In my first week at school, we were informed that we were in 'the top one per cent' in Northern Ireland. This felt good. A few weeks later, the same teacher said, 'God help us, if this is the top one per cent.' This did not feel so good.

The school buildings were an interesting architectural reflection of the history of Belfast. They ranged from eighteenth-century Gothic granite to the 1970s red-brick style peculiar to Belfast, which featured as few breakable windows as possible. There was a swimming pool with no windows that smelt of Domestos and was always too warm. This was where I got my 100-metres front crawl badge and two verrucas, and where I laughed cruelly at Martin Simpson when he still needed armbands in Third Form, which made him cry.

In the most historic part of the school building was the Holy Grail of BRA: the framed charter conveying royal status on the school. The headmaster introduced us to it in our first year, with hushed and reverent tones. I had never seen a royal signature before, although my granny had a mug of Princess Anne's wedding to Captain Mark Phillips. There was nothing in the world more important than being British. It was the opposite of being Irish. It was what you were supposed to kill and die for, although no one ever told me why. And you could hardly get more British than being royal. The Queen and King Billy were both royals, and they were nearly as British as Ian Paisley.

BRA was full of long corridors, which was good when you wanted somewhere quiet to snog a wee girl during lunch break, but bad when you were hurrying to Mr Jackson's maths class, because if you were late, he would rap his knuckles on your head so violently that you would have to try hard not to cry in front of your classmates. Outside the school dining hall, the walls in the corridor were covered with pictures of the glorious First XV rugby team, going back a thousand years. As we queued up for vegetable roll and mash and pink custard, we would examine the pictures from the 1940s, recognising some of our ageing teachers as spotty scrum halves. We debated as to what could possibly have possessed them to come back to teach here.

When it became clear that I would not be following in the studded boot steps of my rugby-playing brother, my form teacher cheerfully informed me that I would therefore be spending the rest of my school years 'in oblivion'. From that day forward, I found it almost impossible to develop an adequate appetite while queuing up for school dinners due to being surrounded by generations of rugger boys smiling smugly down at me. Of course, it could have been much worse, I reasoned. Apparently, there was a wee lad in Second Form who got free school dinners!

I would go on to make friends with kids from up the Antrim Road who lived in detached houses with flowering pink cherry trees, and whose fathers drove Rovers and read clever newspapers like the *Daily Mail*. No one ever ordered the *Daily Mail* up our way. Not one edition of it had ever graced my paperbag. My new-found friends talked about another world – of discos in the Rugby Club, fondue dinner parties and a glass of wine with Sunday lunch. Most of the other kids' dads came to the school concerts, and I noticed when they clapped that they all had very clean hands. A lot of them had good jobs in the bank. Working as a banker was the ultimate job if you weren't smart enough to be a doctor.

Some of my friends' dads even played golf with the teachers. When I enquired of my father why he did not participate in this particular pastime, he replied with some disdain that it was a 'middle-class sport', and that 'no son of his would ever be playing golf'. I added this command to the ever-lengthening list of things that no son of his would ever do, and, interestingly for me this particular forecast turned out to be accurate. 'You're working class and don't you ever forget it, son,' he would often say.

Much as I resented this edict of my father's, at Belfast Royal Academy it was absolutely impossible to forget it. I soon learned the rules. When friends asked me where I lived, I said something vague like, 'On the edge of North Belfast.' This sounded more posh and less Catholic than West Belfast. Sometimes I would say 'Beside the Black Mountain,' as opposed to Divis Mountain, which sounded too much like the notorious Divis Flats. Now and again I would say 'A couple of miles from school,' which was technically true but sufficiently vague to mask my Shankill shame. On the few occasions that I would get a lift to school in our old Ford Escort, and even after the respray, I made sure I got left off around the corner, where no middle-class mate's eyes would spot my modest mode of transport. I once got a lift with a friend from the Antrim Road whose father was a jeweller who drove a BMW. He left us off at the front gates of the school, and I waved goodbye to him as he drove away, with a certain 'he's my father, you know' look on my face. Wee Thomas O'Hara had just got off the bus across the road and observed this pretentious behaviour. He said nothing, just looked straight at me and rolled his eyes.

But bigger circumstances conspired against me, again and again. Street unrest, Ulster Workers' strikes and hunger strikes exposed my secrets at school, as well as disrupting my newspaper deliveries. Being late, or not being able to get to and from school at all because of burning barricades was a bit of a giveaway. Worse still, having to walk to school wearing no school uniform – so as to avoid the danger of having your religion written all over you – tended to expose the secret of the area you lived in. The days that half a dozen kids, usually including Thomas and me, were the only ones in class not in uniform were like those bad dreams where you go to school in your pyjamas.

On one such day, I overheard a cocky classmate, Timothy Longsley, whose brother played in the glorious First XV rugby team, whispering conspiratorially in Chemistry to Judy Carlton (who I fancied): 'He lives in one of those rough areas where the bigots burn the buses, you know.'

'Who do you think you're lookin' at?' I shouted aggressively across the test tubes. I felt like a piece of phosphorous that was just about to ignite in oxygen.

'None of your f**k-ing business!' Timothy snorted back.

He had stabbed me with an obscene 'ing'. His daddy was a lawyer and his mother wore a fur coat and too much make-up at the School Prize Giving, where his brother always got a prize for Latin.

Judy Carlton looked at me sympathetically, but not without a certain sparkle in her lovely blue eyes. I noted this, admired her lips and filed this reaction away for future analysis. I resisted my urge to assault Timothy with a conveniently lit Bunsen burner, as I thought it would just prove his hypothesis. Anyway, I knew this would not be an appropriate course of action for the only pacifist paperboy in West Belfast.

Sometimes it seemed that there were always secrets to be kept, no matter where you went. At orchestra practice at the School of Music on Saturday mornings, I met lots of other Catholic kids who went to grammar schools on the Falls Road. That really threw me. I had assumed that because the Falls was the Catholic version of the Shankill, they wouldn't have grammar schools in their streets either. I didn't know why there were no grammar schools on the Shankill Road. No one seemed to mind anyway.

It was at the School of Music that I met Patrick Walsh. He played the violin better than me, but his voice hadn't broken yet. While I languished in the back row of the second violins, Patrick was given solos at the front of the first violins. He went to St Malachy's Boys Grammar School on the Antrim Road, where priests taught them maths. St Malachy's was the nearest Catholic school to BRA, so the teachers in both establishments arranged that we would never get out of school at the same time: they were afraid, it seemed, of what would happen if we ever met each other. Patrick was from Andersonstown where the IRA ruled and the kerbs were painted green, white and orange — which was the opposite of red, white and blue.

One day, during a break from the musical massacre of one of Beethoven's finer pieces, Patrick asked me, 'Do you go to Belfast Royal Academy?' His lip seemed to curl up slightly as he said the word 'Royal'. I had never heard anyone say 'Royal' before without obvious deference, so I thought this was odd.

'Aye, I go to BRA, so I do,' I replied.

'Are you a ... Prod?' he pressed. Patrick seemed to have difficulty saying the word 'Prod', and there was that lip curl again. He seemed to be upset at me being what I was.

'Aye,' I replied.

'You're rich!' he then squeaked, accusingly.

This was front-page news to me. I was once again confused. At BRA I was poor, but now at the School of Music, just like in the Upper Shankill, I was rich again. And now there was a need for yet another secret. We only met once a week at the School of Music, so I had thought that I wouldn't need to keep any secrets — but now I realised that I would have to keep quiet about being a Shankill paperboy here too.

Patrick however knew the truth, and so he would regularly educate me on a Saturday morning. He said that his father worked at Queen's University, and knew all about being oppressed by the Brits for hundreds of years. He said that I was an Orangeman and that as such I would be handed all the best jobs on a plate. I knew I wasn't an Orangeman because my father kept the Sash his father wore up in the roof space, but Patrick did seem to have a point about all the best jobs, as delivering the papers for Oul' Mac was one of the best jobs around.

One seriously savage afternoon, when all the buses were off and I was definitely going to be late for my papers, our headmaster asked an English teacher from Templepatrick (where the doctors lived) to transport a handful of us safely from the bosom of BRA to the Ballygomartin Road.

'Where's the Ballygomartin Road?' asked the English teacher, to my astonishment. Okay, so it wasn't Shakespeare, but it was only two miles up the road.

'It's an extension of the Shankill Road,' replied the headmaster. It stung to hear my humble origins exposed with such authority. The English teacher's face turned the same colour as his chalky fingers. This surprised me. I couldn't think of a single episode of the Troubles which involved English teachers from Templepatrick being regarded as legitimate targets on the Shankill Road. In Belfast, legitimate targets were more likely to be taxi drivers and milkmen.

The English teacher looked edgy as we crammed into his spotless hatchback, which had Jane Austen on the back seat and a Radio 4 play on the radio. I definitely smelled sweat as he drove us up the Road. He was never this twitchy when teaching us about the war poets, but he put me in mind of those lines from Wilfred Owen when I noticed his 'hanging face, like a devil's, sick of sin'. He was only driving us up the Shankill Road: he wasn't being gassed in the trenches! As the teacher in question transported us silently, I imagined the paperboy from his area, sitting snugly on a brand-new

Chopper bike, and presenting him with a pristine copy of *The Times*. I was sure that his kids in Templepatrick would be getting Eleven Plus practice papers instead of the *Whizzer and Chips*.

The entrance to our estate was up a dark muddy lane. The mothers had been campaigning for a proper road on UTV, but it was still just a mucky path. On one side of the lane was the Girls' Secondary School and on the other side was the Boys' Secondary School. Most of the Shankill went there at eleven years old when they failed the Eleven Plus. Neither school was renowned for academic achievement. My mother always said it was a good thing I hadn't failed my Eleven Plus, because I would have been 'eaten alive in there'. My English teacher must have had similar concerns of being cannibalised as he drove up that dirty dark lane, sandwiched between two staunch secondary schools, for he proceeded with extreme caution. It was like the Doctor leaving the TARDIS for the first time, having just materialised on a strange alien planet.

As he drove along the lane slowly, the teacher at last cut the silence to say, 'This looks like the sort of place they take you in the dark to put a bullet in your head!'

His passengers laughed instantly, but only very briefly, because he didn't join in. We thought he was joking, but of course he wasn't. I, for one, felt offended, and the following year, I resented the same man through every page of *Pygmalion*. Of course, I knew from the front page of the papers every day that people like me and Thomas were getting bullets in their heads just for being Catholics or Protestants from the wrong sort of place. But this was the sort of place I came from, this sort of place was my home, and this was the sort of place where I determinedly delivered forty-eight *Belfast Telegraphs* each night in the darkness.

# CHAPTER FIVE

## *a rival arrives*

I was at the top of my game, the pinnacle of my profession. I had mastered newspaper delivery. No hedge was too high, no letterbox too slim, no holiday supplement too fat and no poodle too ferocious. I had delivered through hail, hoods, bullets and barricades. My paperbag was blacker than anyone else's, the blackest of all paperboys' bags. I had alone survived, when all around me had been robbed or sacked, or both. Oul' Mac even gave me eye contact.

I had achieved high levels of customer satisfaction too. One day, when I was at the doctor's with my mother and a boil on my thigh, we met Mrs Grant, from No. 2, who always gave me a toffee-apple tip at Halloween.

'Your Tony's a great wee paperboy, so he is,' she said, as she darted across the doctor's waiting room, on her way to pick up a prescription for her Richard's chest. The waiting room in the surgery had a shiny old wooden floor that you stared at while you waited, dreading a diagnosis of doom. It smelt of varnish and wart ointment.

'He's the best wee paperboy our street's ever had!' the generous Mrs Grant added. 'He's never late, there's no oul' cheek and he closes the gate.' The whole waiting room stopped coughing, and looked at me admiringly.

'Och, God love the wee crater,' two chirpy old ladies in hats chorused in unison.

This adulation momentarily anaesthetised the pain of my throbbing boil, which had brazenly blossomed on the precise part of my thigh where my paperbag would rub. The word was out: it was official. I was a prince among paperboys. It should have been on the front page of the *Belfast Telegraph* itself.

But then it happened. As unforeseen as a soldier's sudden appearance in your front garden, along came Trevor Johnston. A rival had arrived.

Known to his friends as 'Big Jaunty', Trevor Johnston was older than me, taller than me and cooler than me. He wore the latest brown parallel trousers with tartan turn-ups and a matching brown tank top, from the window in John Frazer's. John Frazer's was the bespoke tailor to the men of the Shankill, whether it was flares, parallels, platform shoes, gargantuan shirt collars or tartan scarves you were after. This emporium of 1970s style was just across the road from the wee pet shop where I got goldfish and tortoises that died, and a mere black-taxi ride down the Shankill Road. From the moment you walked through the front door of the shop and got searched for incendiary devices, you could smell the alluring richness of polyester. It was where I always spent all my Christmas tips.

It seemed that every single time I went to buy some new clothes in Frazer's, there was Trevor Johnston, perusing the parallels. In fact, it was possible that he only left the place during bomb scares. A veritable fashion icon of the Upper Shankill, Trevor also wore a Harrington jacket with the collar turned up. I knew these were very expensive. My big brother had got a Harrington for his birthday, and it

was twenty weeks at 99p from my mother's Great Universal
Club Book. When I said that I wanted one for my birthday
too, my brother tore the page in question out of the Club
Book and fed it to Snowball, our already overweight albino
rabbit. I had to settle for a pair of faux-satin Kung Fu
pyjamas instead. They were twenty weeks at 49p, but I was
determined that my Harrington-jacket day would come.

When Trevor Johnston put all his chic Shankill garments
together, he looked like Eric Faulkner from the Bay City
Rollers, and everybody loved Eric. When I stood beside
Trevor in my duffle coat and grammar-school scarf, I
looked more like Brian Faulkner, the last Prime Minister of
Northern Ireland. And nobody loved him.

One day, without even a five-minute telephone warning,
there was Trevor Johnston, standing with the other
paperboys, waiting for Oul' Mac's van to arrive with the bad
news. Evidently, he had been headhunted at short notice.
The day before, Oul' Mac had sacked Titch McCracken,
who was ginger but good at football like Geordie Best, and
brilliant at twirling his band stick on the Twelfth. Poor wee
Titch had been having a sly smoke in the red telephone box
on our street and had inadvertently dropped a lit match
into his paperbag. Minutes later, the ash of thirty-two *Belly
Tellys* and a half-cremated paperbag on the floor of the
telephone box was all that remained of Titch's career. It had
undoubtedly been the finest fire in our street since the last
Eleventh boney, but Mrs Matchett across the road phoned
the RUC to inform them that the IRA had carried out an
incendiary attack on our telephone box. When Oul' Mac
arrived on the scene, he was so incensed that he couldn't

even speak. This was gross misconduct. Titch was so scared that he couldn't speak either. He knew he was finished. Oul' Mac's disciplinary procedure involved kicking the culprit on the backside halfway up the street, until Titch ran up an entry crying, and from a distance we could hear him telling Oul' Mac where he could stick his paper round.

So, Trevor was here to replace wee Titch. I hated the way all the girls called him 'Big Jaunty', with gormless smiles on their faces. Irene Maxwell — whose da raced pigeons and limped — got a *Jackie* and *Look-in* every week, and so she was something of an authority on matters of art and culture. She once made the momentous prediction that 'them uns from Sweden that won the *Eurovision Song Contest* are going to be more popular than yer man Gary Glitter.'

Every time I arrived at Irene's front gate with her weekly delivery of pop culture, she would gush, 'Big Jaunty's lovely, so he is. He looks like David Cassidy.' One night, I even spotted Irene and her best friend, wee Sandra Hull (who was only six, got a *Twinkle* and permanently had parallel snatter tracks under her nose), following Trevor street by street on his paper round.

Sharon Burgess had never once followed me on my paper round. Living as she did half a mile away, on the other side of the Ballygomartin Road, in one of the clean council houses on the West Circular Road, Sharon never got the chance to revere me at work. Her father was Big Ronnie who riveted in the shipyard, and her mother was Wee Jean who permed pensioners in His n' Hers beside the graveyard.

One Saturday night shortly after the arrival of Trevor Johnston on the paper-delivery scene, I bumped into Sharon at the chippy, with the usual bagful of *Ulsters* on my shoulder. Sharon looked lovely, with her hair flicked like the blonde one in Pan's People on *Top of the Pops*.

'Do you wanna come with me, doin' my *Ulsters*?' I asked romantically, expecting an immediately affirmative response.

'Wise up, wee lad, I'm gettin' a gravy chip and a pastie supper for my da, and *The Two Ronnies* is on our new colour TV the night!' she retorted, devastatingly. Sharon had rejected me for a gravy chip and three old Ronnies! And so no girl had ever followed me and my *Belly Tellys*, just wee hoods and robbers.

Of course, Trevor Johnston looked nothing like David Cassidy. Just because he was the first wee lad in our street to get his hair feathered in His n' Hers didn't mean he looked like a pop star. Who would want to look like David Cassidy anyway? He was crap.

I preferred to call 'Big Jaunty' by his proper name: plain old-fashioned Trevor. I enjoyed that. But I also knew I had to keep well in with him, in spite of everything. Rumour had it that Trevor's da was in the Ulster Volunteer Force, and so it was best not upset him. I noticed that Trevor was the only paperboy who never had so much as an attempted robbery. I didn't know much about the UVF, except that they killed Catholics and beat up burglars. I still couldn't distinguish the difference between the UVF and the UDA, but I reckoned they were a bit like *Shoot* and *Scorcher*, the two main football comics I delivered: they each had different fans, but the same goals. I concluded that they were both just IRAs for Protestants. Trevor's da had big muscles and

UVF tattoos, and wore more gold rings and necklaces than even Mrs Mac. He worked in the foundry with my father, but he seemed to have a lot more money than us. He ran the UVF drinking club down the Road, and I suspected he didn't serve Ulster entirely as a volunteer.

Trevor's da had led the boycott of goods from the South of Ireland in our estate. He put up posters saying: 'Don't Buy Free State Goods' on the same lamp posts the children would swing on. He also promoted his campaign by marching around to everyone's doors and telling my mother and others like her to stop buying Galtee bacon and cheese, because by doing so they were just paying for a United Ireland. Ulster was saying 'No' to Catholic bacon. I hadn't realised the pigs down south were Republicans and even at the age of twelve and a half, I was slightly sceptical as to the purported impact of processed cheese on the constitutional status of Northern Ireland. More importantly, I loved Galtee cheese, especially on a toasted Veda loaf from the Ormo Mini Shop, and I knew my mother snacked on it too while she was watching *Coronation Street*. Once a fortnight Mammy did a surreptitious shop on the Falls Road and would bring home a forbidden block of delicious Galtee from wee Theresa's corner shop. (My mother had sewed trousers with wee Theresa in the suit factory before the Troubles. Apparently she was one of the 'good ones'.) When my granny visited, we would hide the treacherous cheese in the fruit tray at the bottom of the fridge, underneath the oranges, of course.

When I delivered *Muscle Men Monthly* to Trevor's da, there were always men with moustaches and dark glasses smoking in their living room, and I could hear Elvis records playing on the stereogram. Sometimes I wondered why so many Loyalists were Elvis fans: they always seemed more Paisley than Presley to me. There was no obvious connection between the King and the members of the UVF, apart from maybe 'Jailhouse Rock', and even that didn't really make sense, because that was the young, thin Elvis, and these Protestant paramilitaries seemed to like old, fat, white cat-suit Elvis. But maybe Elvis was a Loyalist. Maybe he was doing all those gigs in Las Vegas for the Loyalist prisoners. He could have filled thousands of the collection buckets that came round our door.

One Saturday night, at our local disco, 'the Westy', in a lull between Suzi Quatro and Mudd, I asked Sharon Burgess secretly if she thought Trevor's da was in the UVF. The Westy Disco was a good place to pose such a discreet question, because it was dark and noisy, and no one could hear, or see your eyes.

'Big Jaunty's da?' she replied. 'I don't know, but Big Jaunty's lovely, so he is, he looks like David Cassidy.' I dropped my carton of hot peas and vinegar over the new platform shoes I had just got from John Frazer's.

For six months, Trevor turned up on time and never thieved. He consistently delivered, and was even starting to get some eye contact from Oul' Mac. My position was under threat. The more time I spent with Trevor, the more he irked me.

He was of course the only paperboy with no spots. He never had to use any of his tips to buy a tube of Clearasil which he would have to hide at the back of the bathroom cabinet, behind his father's old Brylcreem jar (that had not been used since he went baldy), in case his big brother found it and accused him of wearing girl's make-up.

I noticed, when we lined up to get the newspapers from Oul' Mac's van, that Trevor always smelled of Brut aftershave – and he hadn't even started shaving! And so it came to pass that Trevor Johnston would be responsible for the most embarrassing incident of my life to date.

Spurred on by jealousy of my rival, I used some of my birthday money to proudly buy my first bottle of Brut from Boots, near the City Hall. I knew that Henry Cooper wore this aftershave, and he had knocked out Muhammed Ali. I only wanted to knock out Trevor Johnston, so I was sure it would do the trick. As I opened my first bottle of Brut, I recalled Henry Cooper in the TV adverts saying that he splashed it all over. The instructions on the bottle itself said the same thing: 'Splash all over.' So that night, as I was getting ready to meet Sharon Burgess, to watch her wee brother play the flute at the band parade, I did just that. By this time, Sharon and I had become an item, much to my great joy.

But no one had warned me that 'all over' should not include your jimmy joe. As the burning sensation increased, I rapidly ran a cold bath, submerged the painful region and sat, shivering and suffering in silence, in the vain hope that no one would notice. My mother's intuition, however, intervened to inform her that something was amiss. Her persistent knocking at the locked bathroom door eventually forced me to admit my error with the aftershave.

'Come on, love, tell me what's wrong,' she pleaded. 'I'm your mammy, love, it's all right.'

'Okay!' I finally confessed. 'I put Brut on my jimmy joe!' I blurted out, 'and it's killin' me!'

Within seconds, Mammy was down the stairs and into the greenhouse in the back garden, where my father was watering his tomatoes.

'Oh my God, Eric, we're gonna have to take our Tony to the Royal! He's put aftershave on his wee jimmy joe!' she shrieked, much, much too loudly.

Could it get any worse? The prospect of being wheeled into Casualty in the Royal with a Brut burn on my jimmy joe was an absolute nightmare. My mother's unnecessary use of the word 'wee' in this context completed my humiliation.

I heard the sound of the watering can clattering on the crazy paving and my father shouting: 'The stupid wee glipe!' But, then to my relief, he added, 'No son of mine will be going to the Royal with an aftershave burn on his ...'

This welcome pronouncement was interrupted by the outbreak of hysterical laugher from the nearby garden shed. My big brother had been in there with my wee brother, teaching him how to play poker with matches, and they had heard everything. The reverberation of their laughter on the shaky wooden walls of the garden shed continued long after the pain had subsided. My wee brother was only six years old at the time, but for weeks afterwards, he replaced 'Humpty Dumpty Sat on a Wall' with a new nursery rhyme, which he chanted again and again, with a delighted chuckle as he bounced up and down the street on his space hopper: 'Our Tony put Brut on his wee jimmy joe / Our Tony put Brut on his wee jimmy joe'.

I was learning that a TV commercial was like the Bible in Belfast: if you took it entirely literally, it could cause a lot of pain. Of course it had all been Trevor Johnston's fault – he had made me do it!

When my rival first arrived to do paper delivery, the pecking order of paperboys was already established. The rule was that when everyone assembled at Oul' Mac's van for the distribution of the papers, the more senior paperboys received theirs first. By this stage, it was I who was in pole position. New boys and younger boys got their newspapers last, even if sometimes these included a couple of torn back pages for which they would have to suffer the consequences from an angry customer who played the Football Pools. The shade of the paperbags slung on the shoulders of the line-up of paperboys painted a spectrum of power and status. At the front, almost head to head with Oul' Mac, were the dirtiest bags, while the clean bags loitered nervously at the back. To my horror, after a few months of Trevor being in his employ, and twice in one week, Oul' Mac gave him his papers first. This was getting serious! Maybe Mrs Mac hadn't cleaned Oul' Mac's glasses that month, or maybe he was confused by the smell of all that Brut, I hoped desperately, clinging to the possibility of some sensory impairment on Mac's part as an explanation.

Suddenly, Trevor Johnston was everywhere, like little Jimmy Osmond. He was even in my scout troop! And when he was made the leader of my patrol group just because he was tall and good at knots, I was livid. As we lined up, raised three fingers to God and the Queen and said, 'Dib, dib, dib', Trevor was at the top. Big Jaunty was the leader of the pack.

Then, one Friday night, I was delivering the *Jackie* to Irene Maxwell. I had struggled to remove the white knitting

wool tied round the gate and gatepost to stop Irene's wee
brother from getting out onto the road, so I was already
distracted. When I removed the glossy magazine from the
grimy interior of my paperbag, there was David Cassidy
on the cover.

'He looks a bit like Big Jaunty, so he does,' I found
myself thinking, before catching myself on. It was the last
straw. I snapped like one of my guitar strings being tuned
too tightly. I hated Trevor Johnston! I wanted him to try
to jump Mr Hamilton's fence and catch his Doc Marten
laces on the wire, and fall on his pretty face and tear his
parallels at the knees and to have to get stitches in the Royal.
I knew the only pacifist paperboy in West Belfast should not
be thinking this way, but then again, most people in Belfast
were justifying much worse.

However, fate was to intervene, as generously as a drunk
customer deciding to tip on a Christmas Eve. It was just a
couple of weeks before the banging of the bin lids for the
anniversary of Internment, and my mother was standing at
our front gate, shouting up the street at me that my dinner
was ready. I had just finished the papers, and, as I arrived
at the merciless and still unforgiven, guitar-abusing gate,
who should be striding up the street towards our house but
Trevor's da! He always looked like he was marching, even
when it wasn't the Twelfth.

'Doesn't his son do the papers with you, love?' my
mother asked and added, innocently, 'You know, Big
Jaunty – he looks like the lovely wee fella that sings on the
Partridge Family, so he does.' I gripped my paperbag strap
and breathed deeply.

'Hello, Mr Johnston, what about ye? It would melt ye the day,' Mammy said, alluding to the fine summer weather.

'Och, Betty love, what about ye?' he replied. 'Isn't it terrible what them Fenians are tryin' til do til us?'

'Och aye, terrible, love,' she complied.

This was like talking about the weather to Trevor's da.

'I hope you're not buying any more of that Papish cheese?' he continued.

'Wouldn't touch it, love,' lied my mother impressively.

Just then, I noticed an unfamiliar feeling of warmth in my Doc Martens – and I knew it couldn't have been coins, as it wasn't a Friday night. I looked down to see that Trevor's da's dog had just peed on my boots. It was a yappy wee chihuahua, which was quite surprising because most of the Loyalist leadership had rottweilers. My big brother said men who walked chihuahuas were homos, just like wee lads who played violins. (He added this second fact just to peeve me, of course.) According to my big brother, there was only one thing in the world worse than being a Provo, and that was being a homo. I sometimes wondered what he would do if he ever met a homo Provo. I thought homos were boys who wanted to kiss boys, and that had nothing to do with either small dogs or musical instruments. I myself only wanted to kiss Sharon Burgess, and I couldn't imagine Trevor's da kissing one of his mates with a moustache in the UVF.

'Have you heard our news?' asked Trevor's da.

'No, love,' said my mother, 'Is your Martha bad with her nerves again?'

'No, Betty, love, we're movin' to Bangor.'

'Yes!' I almost leapt out of my squelching boots.

Bangor was on the train by the sea, and where you moved if you got a good job in the bank. We used to go to there on the Sunday-school excursion, but we had to sing 'Jesus Loves Me' and not 'The Sash' on the double-decker. Bangor had a Barry's Amusements that still used old money like my granny: halfpennies, pennies and sixpences. The dodgems didn't do decimal. Barry's also had an old ghost train that was scary but not frightening. It was a safe sort of scary, not like getting a bus in Belfast in the riots.

Bangor also had a very famous outdoor swimming pool called Pickie Pool, where, as my parents told me, they would go for a paddle when they were courting. I never got a go in it because I always forgot my rubber ring. Of course, Big Jaunty wouldn't need any inflatable assistance once he got there. He was probably a brilliant swimmer, like yer man Mark Spitz with the moustache, from the Olympics!

My mother was genuinely shocked by Trevor's da's revelation.

'Och, I'm sorry to hear your news, love. When are yousens leavin'?' she enquired.

This was breaking news, and I could tell she was determined to get all the details before Big Aggie up the street, who was jealous of her sewing and usually uncovered the best gossip first.

'September, love. Martha says it's not the same round here since all the dirt from down the Road are movin' up, and she says our Trevor would be far better off in Bangor with his asthma, and it's got one of them new shopping centres.'

As he marched off down the street, I'm sure I heard

my mother say something under her breath, like, 'I'm sure they'll be delighted in Bangor.'

Afterwards, Mum rushed the fish fingers and Smash 'potatoes', and disappeared for most of the evening. Later, as I ran around the corner to the erstwhile telephone box towering inferno, with two 2p pieces in my hand to listen to the new Showaddywaddy single on Dial-a-Disc, I spotted my mother still sprinting from house to house like a good paperboy, conveying the news to the most trusted neighbours. She was clearly enjoying delivering these tidings. Sadly, I had to hang up on Dial-a-Disc after the first chorus of 'Under the Moon of Love', because my big brother walked past and overheard me singing along, and shouted through one of the many broken windows: 'Are you singing down the phone to Sharon Burgess, ya big fruit?!'

As I stomped home in humiliation, I noticed as I looked down that the white ash from Titch's papers was now covering my Doc Martens, due to the adhesive properties of Trevor's da's dog's pee. It was, I imagined, just like the layer of ash from Pompeii in my school history book. As I looked for a convenient pavement puddle to clean it off my boots, I noticed Irene Maxwell standing at her gate, crying her eyes out.

'What's the matter with you, Irene?' I asked. She could hardly splutter the words out through the sobs, but I knew what was coming next anyway.

'Big Jaunty's leavin' to live in Bangor, and he was lovely, so he was, and he looked like David Cassidy and ... and I think I love him,' she wailed.

'Now she sounds like a David Cassidy song herself,' I thought, unsympathetically.

Then I did two sins I had been told not to do. Uncle John at the Good News Club had told me not to tell lies, and my father had told me not to be such a selfish wee bastard. To my shame, I did both simultaneously, with a heartbroken Irene Maxwell.

'Och, isn't that awful?' I feigned. 'I hadn't heard he was leavin' and Big Jaunty was one of my best paperboy mates too. Oul' Mac'll be ragin', so he will, and – oh no, I might have to be the new patrol leader in the Scouts!'

My thoughtless words only compounded Irene's grief, and so I made a stab at consoling her: 'Sure, you and wee Sandra might see him at Pickie Pool on the Sunday-school excursion next year. Although I heard Trevor's mammy doesn't let him go out much, because he's bad with his asthma.'

Poor Irene. I handed her my other two pence and told her not to worry, because Showaddywaddy's new single was brilliant and that she should go and listen to it on Dial-a-Disc round in the telephone box, but that she should watch her sandals, because the ash from Titch's paperbag was still on the floor.

I was as heartless as an apprentice petrol-bomber but happier than a paperboy sent home on full pay because Oul' Mac's van was hijacked. Trevor would be transferred to a North Down newsagent, and he would take his brown parallels with the tartan turn-ups and his feathered hair and his inflammatory Brut with him to Bangor. And all the girls at Pickie Pool would say Big Jaunty was lovely, so he was, and that he looked like David Cassidy, but I wouldn't have to care anymore!

After six months of serious challenge, I was to be peerless and without equal once more – undisputedly, the top paperboy in the Upper Shankill.

# CHAPTER SIX

## *three steps to heaven*

Weekends were hard work for a paperboy, so they were. There wasn't just the gauntlet of Friday nights to be run, with the possibility of attacks by wee hoods hopeful of stealing your takings for the week: on Saturdays, there were heavy additional professional demands too. Saturday night meant two newspapers to be delivered, and so double the weekday workload. There was *Ireland's Saturday Night* as well as that day's edition of the *Belfast Telegraph*. The former was very popular in the Upper Shankill, even though it had 'Ireland' in the title. Of course, you weren't supposed to like anything with Ireland in the title (although the Church of Ireland seemed to be all right for some people). I remember us all having to cheer very quietly the night Dana – who said she was from 'Derry' instead of 'Londonderry' – won the Eurovision Song Contest for Ireland. If Mrs Piper had heard us cheering because of 'All Kinds of Everything' getting 'douze points' from Norway, she might very well have suspected that we were secret IRA supporters and we could have ended up by getting a 'friendly' call from Trevor's da.

Anyway, for some strange reason, *Ireland's Saturday Night* was known to everyone as the *Ulster*. In my younger days, I had thought that the Shankill was Ulster. Later I realised the Shankill was in Ulster. Then, in geography class one day, I noticed on the map that Ulster was in Ireland. Finally, I learned that, although Ulster was not actually in Britain, it was, in fact, more British than Britain itself. It all made perfect sense. The *Ulster* newspaper was simple too. It was a straightforward weekly sports paper with all the day's sporting results. Published on a Saturday evening, to catch all the latest sports results from matches and races that had taken place earlier in the day, it was a true 'hot-off-the-presses' newspaper.

You felt special delivering the *Ulster*, because people were standing in the street waiting for it. You were a very important person, because you were the courier of extremely valuable information: you had something fresh and precious, something everyone wanted now. With the *Ulsters* slung over my shoulder, I felt like a scout from a John Wayne movie, returning to the circled wagons to tell his compatriots where the Apaches were. Men who liked football and horses got the *Ulster*, and they often met me at their front door to take delivery of it. They were like kids getting a birthday card or their Eleven Plus results, or like Irene Maxwell getting her *Jackie* when it had David Cassidy on the front. These customers would start reading the paper straight away, standing up, fully absorbed in its contents, even before the front door was shut again.

All of this was, however, a mystery to me. I couldn't imagine a more boring newspaper, apart from that pink English newspaper with all the numbers in it, which nobody up our way ever got. I myself preferred to read about *Space 1999* and *The Tomorrow People* in *Look-in* magazine. Science fiction was so much more exciting than football, and it seemed to cause less trouble, even though there was usually a higher body count. Unlike with football, Protestants and Catholics seemed to like the same science-fiction programmes. No one ever rioted after an episode of *Lost in Space*, even when Dr Zachary Smith had endangered the life of Will Robinson and his family yet again!

I had sixteen *Ulsters* to dispatch on a Saturday evening. This wasn't very many, relatively speaking, but though it didn't take long to deliver them, it did tend to mess up my social life if I was planning to meet Sharon Burgess at the Westy Disco on a Saturday night.

The Westy Disco was so called because it was a disco that was held in a hut on the corner of the West Circular Road. It was an old Nissen hut from the war which was used by Ballygomartin Presbyterian as a church hall, falling down and freezing though it was. I went to our well-ordered Scouts meetings there when the lights were on, but on a Saturday night the hut was transformed, and the lights were switched off and replaced by flashing coloured spotlights and ultraviolet tubes that made your white socks and dandruff glow in the dark. I always made sure to wash my hair with Head & Shoulders before a night out at the Westy Disco, because there was nothing as humiliating as wee girls laughing at your fluorescent dandruff as you tried to do a manly dance to Status Quo.

Every Saturday night, all of us teenagers crammed into that ageing Nissen hut, as the corrugated iron walls vibrated to the sounds of the latest hits from Sweet and The Glitter Band. The floor was sticky with chewing gum and slippy with condensation, but we managed to make our moves anyway – the Slush, the Twist, the Bump and the Hucklebuck. We had to, because this was our only dance floor. The Westy Disco certainly attracted far more kids than Sunday school or the Scouts. Some nights, there were more than four hundred of us in platforms and parallels, dancing innocently to Showaddywaddy and the Bay City Rollers, while outside our city convulsed.

The Westy was a good place to ask a wee girl you fancied for a slow dance during a Donny Osmond song, so that you could have a go at snogging. It was here in the dark that I discovered that tongues could have more fun than just blowing bubble gum. Of course, some of the people in the church who never smiled did not approve of such worldly discos. They said that dancing was a sin, because it was like sex. It surprised me that sex was a sin. I was certain that even good livin' people did it, because they had lots of kids and not all of them could have been adopted. However, Reverend Lowe, our independently minded minister, allowed us to dance because, as he said, it kept us off the dangerous streets and out of the pubs and the paramilitary organisations. On several occasions, Reverend Lowe had been spotted ordering paramilitaries off the dangerous streets into the pubs. He used to preach about the lesser of two evils.

I, however, was no ordinary member of the Westy Disco. I was in a very privileged position. My parents were voluntary youth leaders, in charge of the most popular youth gathering in the whole Shankill. This made me special: it was like being one of Paul and Linda McCartney's children. My parents had started the disco, along with Uncle Henry and Auntie Emma from our street. (They weren't my real aunt and uncle, but they were warm people, and just like family to us.) Uncle Henry did the door where we paid our 10p and blew into the breathalyser to get in. My mother and Auntie Emma, who were best friends and like mammys to the whole hut, did the tuck shop where you could get crisps and chewing gum, and peas and vinegar. Auntie Emma never missed a Saturday night, even though she didn't like the disco lights because the ultraviolet rays made her prematurely false teeth look black. Uncle Henry was the warm heart of the Westy, but it was my father who was the star. Daddy was the DJ, like Jimmy Savile on *Top of the Pops*, only younger. He played the 45s on a double-deck turntable plugged into enormous speakers and would turn up the music so loud that the neighbours would complain. This was very cool, of course: not many dads up our way got accused of blaring out the Rollers too loud.

As resident DJ at the Westy, my father picked the hits and read out the requests, so he did. With the profits from the tuck shop, he would buy two new singles every week from the record store. They were the latest new releases, and they would be his Top 40 predictions: he always managed to choose the songs that went to No.1. My father was an unlikely candidate for youth-club leader in the church, because he wasn't 'good livin'' at all. He smoked and drank and said God didn't exist because Christians didn't practise what they preached. I wasn't so sure that this followed, because paperboys often didn't do what they were commanded to do either, but Oul' Mac certainly still existed.

For a middle-aged man, Da's musical choices were very good, although he did get a little too excited by some of the

more irritating Boney M singles. One of them was called
'Belfast': it was a bouncy little singalong pop song all about
our hatred for one another in our city. We danced and sang
along to it as if it was about something happy and funny,
like 'Waterloo'. I put my position as son of the DJ to good
use, slipping in extra requests for my latest favourite singles
and asking my da to play slow songs by Donny Osmond at
just the right moment, when Sharon Burgess might be most
receptive.

One of the best slow songs that often elicited a snog from
your girl was 'Three Steps to Heaven' by Showaddywaddy.
The lyrics were brilliant. They gave you an easy-to-
remember, step-by-step guide to getting yourself a girl.
Showaddywaddy were geniuses. Unfortunately Mrs Piper
disagreed, and when she heard this song blaring out while
passing the hut on the way to her prayer meeting one night,
she complained to my father for leading us all astray with
'the Devil's music'. She said that there was only one true
step to heaven and that was for us all to get saved. My DJ da
told her to catch herself on.

Whatever Mrs Piper thought, I followed Showaddywaddy's instructions to the letter. 'And as I travel on and
things do go wrong ....' they sang. It was as if they knew
of my personal travel problems due to all the buses getting
hijacked in Belfast! 'Just call it steps one, two and three,'
they crooned, and I would listen with an earnest desire to
follow these 'three steps to heaven', so I would. 'Step One
– to find a girl to love ...' Sharon Burgess, of course. 'Step
Two – she falls in love with you ...' Hopefully – if I have
splashed enough Brut all over. 'Step Three - you kiss and

hold her tightly ...' Yes! A proper snog like Big Ruby at the caravan had shown me. 'That sure feels like heaven to me.'

The night at the Westy Disco always ended with 'The Last Waltz' by Engelbert Humperdinck. When the first bars of the piano commenced, we knew it was time for a fish supper and perhaps the opportunity to walk a girl home. Engelbert certainly cleared the floor, because 'The Last Waltz' was old-fashioned compared to the latest number from The Rubettes, but I knew this tune also had a deeper meaning. It was my parents' favourite song from the stereogram in the sitting room, and the one to which they had danced when they won the Ballroom Dancing Competition at Butlin's in Mosney the year before. So Da played it every week, not just to let us all know that the disco was over but also to let my mother know that he loved her.

In terms of paper delivery, the mountain had to go to Mohammed on a Saturday evening. Oul' Mac didn't deliver the *Ulsters* to the streets in the legendary yellow van, as was his wont on week nights. He had clearly carried out a cost–benefit analysis on using the van for such a relatively small delivery. The executive summary of this time-and-motion study was communicated to us in no uncertain terms: 'Youse can come and get the *Ulsters* yerselves, ya lazy wee buggers,' he advised. So on Saturdays I had to walk to Oul' Mac's shop, down at the bottom of the Ballygomartin Road. This was more of a nuisance than a heavy burden until one Saturday night, when something happened which would henceforth give my favourite Showaddywaddy song a whole new meaning.

On the dark Saturday night in question, I am on my

way home from the newsagents with my *Ulsters*. It is late
October. I have already emptied my boots of the takings
from late-paying customers and handed over the warm and
fragrant coins to Mrs Mac. I have bought myself a packet
of sweetie mice with a tip from Mrs Hill with the baldy
poodle. Walking back up the hill towards my street, I hear
the customary noise of a bomb thudding somewhere in the
city. It is not too loud this time, not like the night the IRA
blew up the Gasworks and the whole sky lit up like in a
crash landing from *Lost in Space*.

It is the first frost of October. Icy footpaths are brilliant
for sliding on, except when your bag is so heavy that you lose
balance, and your fall shreds the sports pages of the papers
you are carrying, and No. 93, who never tips, complains,
and Oul' Mac shouts that you are a 'clumsy wee hallion'. I
can see my breath in the cold stillness. I recognise a frosty,
smoky Halloween smell in the air: fog and sparklers. I am
happy, as usual. As I walk past the chippy, my mouth waters
at the wafting aroma of fish suppers on the vinegar-soaked
pages of the papers I had delivered yesterday. I am alone, my
ever darker paperbag over my shoulder, my fingers yet again
black with ink from troubled pages.

All at once, I become aware of two men, walking close
behind me. I glance around. One of them looks like the lead
singer in Showaddywaddy, yer man with the dark glasses.
The other, smaller, one has an aggressive mouth like a dog
that bites paperboys, and he looks like he's had too many
fish suppers. They are both staring at me in an unmistakable,
'hard man' way. I am outnumbered, so I don't even dare to
venture a 'who d'ye think yer lookin' at?'

'Robbers!' I conclude in a tense instant, although these are guys in their twenties – older than the usual robbers. Their pace has now quickened, as if they are trying to catch up with me. I quickly turn off the main Ballygomartin Road to escape into an empty street and up the hill towards home. Safety always seems to be hillwards in these parts. The two men follow.

In my mind, all I can hear is the robot in *Lost in Space* repeating, 'Danger, Will Robinson! Danger, Will Robinson! Danger, Will Robinson!'

Catching up, my pursuers bundle me into the small untidy front garden at No. 4, whose owners are never in, but who always get the *Radio Times* (I always read it in the street when *DoctorWho* is on the cover). The Showaddywaddy guy presses something hard and cold into my back through my duffle coat. 'Danger, Will Robinson! Danger, Will Robinson!'

I hear metal clicks against my toggles as I struggle and turn to get loose. I bite on my grammar-school scarf.

'I don't have any money,' I cry, my newly broken voice returning to prepubescent shrillness. I am telling the truth. My boots are empty. Instinctively, I then turn out my pockets. There is no money, just the remains of a melting white sweetie mouse encrusting a bull's-eye marble. My assailants don't seem interested.

They don't speak. I freeze. I don't understand. 'They are IRA men after an easy target,' I fret inwardly. 'Danger, Will Robinson! Danger, Will Robinson!'

It starts to rain very heavily. Icy drops dilute the warm tears on my shivering cheeks. Suddenly, Mr Watson with the dyed black comb-over from No. 24 – whose wife gets

*Woman* and who always gives a big tip at Easter — comes running down the street towards us. My oppressors see him coming, and mistakenly sense an attempted rescue. The tough guys just run off. But Mr Watson is just running to escape the downpour of hail. I stand alone in the trampled weeds of the garden of No. 4 beside a small gnome with a fishing rod and his nose broken off. Mr Watson runs straight past me. He has tonight's *Belfast Telegraph* over his head to protect his much-too-black Brylcreemed hair.

I must run home. But, I then remember, no one is at home. I must run to the Westy Disco, where Dad will be playing 'Mamma Mia' and Mum will be clipping Geordie Cooper around the ear for stealing penny chews, as per usual. I must tell them what has just happened. I can't catch a breath. I can't speak. They had put a gun in my back. I start to hyperventilate. (I thought only Americans hyperventilated.) I burst into the Westy Disco before Uncle Henry can even breathalyse me. A group of adults and wee girls gather around me at the tuck shop. I am crying. Then I am embarrassed: what if Sharon Burgess sees me like this?

The mood of the tuck-shop crowd surrounding me changes from concern, to shock and then to outrage. Meanwhile, Geordie Cooper empties the penny-chew jar behind them all.

The general consensus is that the IRA has just tried to kill me.

'Them f**kin' Provos have just tried to a pick off another wee Prod the night!' shouts Philip Ferris insensitively. The rumour spreads across the dance floor that paperboys are now 'legitimate targets'. Then I notice the muffled sounds of

Showaddywaddy from the loudspeakers in the background – it's 'Three Steps to Heaven'. The lyrics mock me. I feel as if I have just taken several steps closer to heaven than I had ever wanted to.

Within twenty-four hours, I am in Tennent Street police station with my father and a serious-looking young policeman with a moustache, called Darren. (All the RUC men have moustaches, and many of them are called Darren.) I feel more unsafe inside the RUC station than when I was cornered in a garden by the Showaddywaddy guy, because the Provos keep attacking the Tennent Street station with mortar bombs, and even though the building is surrounded by concrete and fencing nearly as tall as a peace wall, the mortars always get through. I pray the Provos haven't planned an attack while I am giving my statement.

Constable Darren shows me black-and-white pictures of hard men, the way they do in *Starsky and Hutch*, except these guys are all white. None of them looks like the Showaddywaddy guy, and they all look the same to me: scowling faces, long hair and sideburns like Elvis. I conclude that all criminals have sideburns in the same way that all policemen have moustaches, and that this distinctive use of facial hair is why they find it so easy to avoid one another. I point to the one who looks most like my attacker.

'No, he's in the Maze, son,' says Darren the policeman. Then he asks me if they touched me anywhere. I don't understand the question. They stuck a gun in my back: what could be worse than that? As we leave the RUC station, my father tells me that if I should ever set eyes on those two again, I must tell him right away, and that he would 'take care of the bastards'. I can foresee another outing for the pickaxe handle, but I'm not so sure it would do the job this time.

* * *

A few months after this, I was waiting on the Ballygomartin Road for the No. 73 bus across town. It was a slippy Saturday morning. The No. 73 said 'Malone' on the front, when on its way into town, and 'Springmartin via Shankill' on the way back. I liked the idea of being on the bus to posh Malone, where my orthodontist lived – but I wondered what the people from over there thought about having to get a rough Springmartin bus into town. But perhaps they didn't get the bus.

I was carrying my violin case this time, instead of my dirty paperbag. My fingertips were sore from last-minute practice. I had string-imprinted fingers and coin-embossed toes! I was on my way to the School of Music for orchestra practice, the only boy from this neck of the woods to go there. I had decided never to reveal to the other second violins that I was a Shankill paperboy. Most of them were Catholic grammar-school girls, and I fancied one of them, a dark-haired girl with a cello and an Irish name I couldn't spell. But I knew the rules: I was the wrong sort from the wrong kind of place. So I settled for a distant admiration of her vibrato. Of course, I didn't tell the other paperboys about the School of Music, either. I knew the combination of mixing with 'Fenians' and playing 'poofy' classical music would attract double derision from them.

The bus was late. I wondered if it had been hijacked – but it was a bit early in the day for hijackers. Then, from across the deserted misty road, an old Ford Cortina pulled up abruptly in front of me. It was the Showaddywaddy guy with the gun. He just sat and stared at me. 'Danger, Will Robinson! Danger, Will Robinson!'

Old Mrs McCready from No. 25, who always got *The Sunday Post*, arrived beside me at the bus stop, rummaging through her old-lady-shopping trolley bag. She didn't even notice yer man, who continued to just sit and stare at me. I wondered what he was going to do this time. I was a teenager now, with a broken voice and getting taller. I still wasn't a fighter, but I had by now learned a fairly effective 'hard-man' stare myself that worked with some of the rugby-playing bullies in school. I wasn't sure if it would work with big lads with guns, but I attempted to stare back convincingly. It is possible that carrying a violin undermined the hard-man stare, but then again, gangsters in old black-and-white movies always looked quite threatening while carrying violin cases, though of course they didn't wear duffle coats and grammar-school scarves.

After what seemed like an endless five minutes, the Showaddywaddy guy simply sneered and drove off, giving me an 'I-know-where-you-live' kind of stare. However, even though I thought about him often after that, I never saw him again. The No. 73 eventually arrived, and I 'dinged' my ticket and sat down with my violin case on my knee, shaking a little. I could hear my bow rattling inside. I wasn't going to tell my father. I didn't want him to take care of yer man, because that would mean someone would then take care of my dad. That's how it worked in Belfast. We were going nowhere – the tit-for-tat mindset reigned supreme.

As we travelled down the Shankill Road, the bus driver turned up his wireless. It was Big T on Downtown Radio – he was always on Downtown on Saturday mornings, when you were having an Ulster fry. He was playing Showaddywaddy: they were singing 'Three Steps to Heaven'. I shivered, so I did.

# CHAPTER SEVEN

## *tips and investments*

'Money, Money, Money' was never off the radio. 'It's a rich man's world!' sang ABBA.

In church, however, when I wasn't daydreaming about Agnetha during the sermon, I heard Reverend Lowe teach an alternative message: that money couldn't make you happy. Although there was evidence before us that the happiest people in our congregation seemed to be the two jolly ladies with thick make-up and bright red lipstick who sat at the front in fur coats. They didn't live up our way anymore but came back in their Jaguar once a week to go to church. When they opened their blue Presbyterian hymn books, I could make out, from where we sat at the back of the church, big gold rings on their plump fingers. I also noticed that Reverend Lowe always gave those fleshy hands an extra strong handshake when we all queued up to exchange a few words with him at the church door at the end of every Sunday morning service.

'They're real ladies and they're very good givers,' Uncle Henry once remarked. He counted the church collection.

My father constantly reminded me that I was working class and should be very proud that we had no money. 'No son of his was ever going to get above himself' was another of his usual refrains. So, when I joined the nation's workforce as a paperboy, I didn't dare tell Daddy that I felt very well off indeed. Not only did I get pocket money every Friday night, and extra pocket money if there was overtime at the foundry, but I also earned £1.50 per week from Oul' Mac, and on top of that I got tips. If you performed your duties well and with a smile, you could, I quickly realised, end up with more tips than wages. I soon learned the earning potential of providing a first-class service with a charming smile. Part of my brain had also developed a highly sensitive 'tip detector'.

Apart from the more obviously promising tipping scenarios – such as holiday times or when the distinctive smell of Tennant's Lager could be detected on the breath of the customer in question – I was soon able to discern, from the use of certain words, the likelihood of potential additional earnings. 'Sorry, I've nothing smaller, love,' for example, signalled a healthy tip. This was the 'no change, big tip' scenario. On one such occasion, Mrs Grant from No. 2 told me to keep the change from a ten-pound note. I was aghast at her generosity, but spent the rest of the evening planning what I would do with the money. Then, the next day, she asked me for a fiver back: she had, she said, made a mistake because her nerves were bad with her Richard's pains. So I had to postpone my plans for a fishing rod and an Etch-a-Sketch.

'Thanks for keepin' an eye on pussy over the Twelfth, love,' also signalled that a good tip was on the cards. This fell into the category of the 'additional duties' related tip, and was most commonly bestowed by pet owners during the month of July. This was easy money because the cats didn't seem to care much if their owners never returned from the caravan.

'Was them robbers at you again the night, love?' or, 'Och, look at the state of you the night in the rain, ya wee crater,' were also promising remarks, indicating an imminent sympathy tip. I accepted such tips with sad and grateful eyes and closed the gate carefully behind me. Then they would go straight to my boots.

Like the baddies in *Thunderbirds* that I could always recognise from the stubble on their plastic faces, I instinctively understood who would never tip. Mr Black always had a 'don't-you-bloody-well-think-you're-getting-an-extra-penny-out-of-me,-ya-cheeky-wee-hallion' look on his face on a Friday night, and never tipped.

So, the identity of a possible tip-giver was predictable. The amount and occasion of a tip, however, was as difficult to foresee as the number of milk-bottle tops donated to the *Blue Peter* appeal for Africa in any given week. This element of uncertainty turned the whole tipping experience into something of an adventure. It was like snow on the streets: you never knew how much you were going to get and when exactly you would get it, but once you knew it was on the way, a whole new world of opportunities for having fun was opened up to you.

The sum of my pocket money, wages and tips was sometimes as much as £4 by the time it was Saturday night. I was rich! Patrick Walsh at the School of Music said all Protestants were rich and that we kept all the Catholics poor. I wasn't so sure, because I had seen a picture of the Pope's church in Rome on *John Craven's Newsround*, and it was even bigger than Ian Paisley's church on the Ravenhill Road. However, I couldn't really argue with Patrick, not just because he was a first violin and I was only a second, but because I was probably the only Protestant he had ever met, and I had to admit that I was very rich for my age.

However, I tried not to flaunt my wealth, and I learned to use it wisely. I invested a few pounds every month into my Abbey National savings account, where you got ten pence for free at the end of every year just for keeping your money there. The Abbey National was on Royal Avenue in the city centre, beside the Grand Central hotel where the army lived, so it got burnt and bombed quite a few times. In spite of this precarious location, the place was always open with a 'Business as Usual' sign and a spirited smell of wet smoke. It felt good, queuing up there to make my deposits alongside adults with wallets and purses. The lady behind the counter wore make-up and pearl earrings, talked through her nose and pronounced every 'ing' as she cheerily accepted all of my investments and firmly stamped my book. The Abbey National savings book had a blue cover like a Presbyterian hymn book, except with a powerful plastic smell. It was the aroma of wealth.

My very first account was for saving up for big expensive things, like a new pair of parallels out of John Frazer's or my ticket for the Bay City Rollers Concert. However, because I was so well-heeled (in platforms of course), I was able to avail of other opportunities for spending my additional disposable income. I quickly learned the hard way though not to play the slot machines in Millisle and not to play poker with my big brother in the shed. I was not prepared to risk losing my hard-earned cash so easily, and also my granny said gambling was a curse and a sin. (This moral outrage about gambling must have put a strain on her marriage, because

Granda worked in the bookies on the Donegall Road.) I gave some of my money away to babies in Africa of course, but I still had enough left to invest in all sorts of exciting products.

So I turned to *Look-in*, my favourite magazine full of interviews, crosswords and pin-ups of the Bionic Woman and the Bay City Rollers. The back pages of this wondrous publication had adverts for an array of investment opportunities for a boy of my means that were not readily available from the shops on the Shankill Road. The lack of local consumer choices on the Shankill Road was regularly confirmed by adults all around me, in fact. 'The Road's nat what it used til be for shappin' no more,' they would say.

So every week, when the magazines arrived in Oul' Mac's shop, I grabbed a *Look-in* and scoured these appealing back-page adverts. I found stamps and books and card collections and strange creatures to buy – all for the cost of a 50p postal order. First of all, I became a member of the Imperial Stamp Club, and got a new set of stamps every month to add to my collection. I got a red stamp collector's book for Christmas and began to stick stamps in the appropriate page for each country. I had never heard of some of the countries and had to look them up in my father's 1959 *Pears Cyclopaedia*. Sometimes my father brought home a bag of old stamps from the war he had borrowed from the foundry, and I added these into my growing collection too. After several messy mistakes, I concluded that I should not attempt to stick stamps in my album immediately after doing the papers, as my inky fingers would soil the crisp white pages. From time to time, I borrowed the *Stamp Valuation Book* out of the Shankill Library (along with a *Billy Bunter* or a *Famous Five*). I would search through the catalogue to discover the invariably disappointing value of each stamp.

Next, I invested in a card collection of animals of the world. For a 50p postal order, I got ten animals a month to put in a wee red card container. My favourite card was the one with the skunk. I dreamed of having a pet skunk to come with me on my paper round on a Friday night and spray foul smells on the foul wee hoods. I cancelled my subscription after about sixty animals however, because I was being sent far too many farm animals. 'Next, they'll be sending me a card of Petra,' I thought. I was very fond of Petra, who was the most popular golden labrador in the Upper Shankill (even if she did poop on all the pavements), but I wanted to collect rare, dangerous, poisonous animals from, say, Borneo – not pets or farm animals from Ballymena. I knew I was the only pacifist paperboy in West Belfast, but I had no ethical difficulty with killer animals, because they didn't seem to know any better.

Inevitably, therefore, I moved on from animal cards and joined the Puffin Book Club, to collect books instead. I hadn't fully realised that you could actually buy your own books – I thought you just borrowed them from school or from the Shankill Library. As a member of the Puffin Book Club, I got a set of book labels saying, 'This book belongs to ...' to stick into the inside cover of every book I bought. I would get very excited when my latest book would arrive. I cherished the smell when you opened the first page for the first time. I started with *The Lion, the Witch and the Wardrobe*, and eventually blew all my tips on Narnia. C.S. Lewis took me away to another land, one where they listened to the children and the baddies didn't rule forever.

I was very proud of my stamp, animal and Narnia collections, but not all of my purchases proved so satisfying. One day, at the back of a *Look-in* summer special, I spotted an advert for 'sea monkeys'. A 50p postal order would buy me a packet of dried sea-monkey eggs, it seemed. If I simply added water, these tiny alien-like creatures would hatch in a jam jar in my bedroom just like magic, and I could raise whole families of them!

I was attracted to the mystery of this new species, and amazed that I could afford them with my tips. Once the sea monkeys arrived, in a very small packet, I followed all of the instructions carefully. After an initial panic on my part that the creatures had perished in the post, sure enough, they hatched within a few days. Unfortunately however, the 'sea monkeys' – despite their exotic name – weren't anything like the families of winged aliens pictured in the *Look-in* advert. They were more like the wee flies you got in rock pools at the seaside when you were looking for crabs and dropped your net, slipping on the seaweed and scraping your knees.

In spite of my disappointment, I acknowledged that the sea monkeys were still God's wee creatures, so I cared for my charges like any responsible parent. Then one sad day while I was watching Rolf Harris painting a kangaroo on BBC 1, my wee brother (inspired by Rolf) used my sea monkeys' jam jar for dipping his paintbrush, so that he could fill in Noddy in his colouring book. My erstwhile pets were permanently preserved as flecks in the red paint on

the bonnet of Noddy's car. However, given the poor return
on this investment, my grief was fairly short-lived. And
my wee brother reminded me that although he had indeed
made a tragic error, it wasn't half as bad as putting Brut on
your jimmy joe.

Shortly after I had recovered from the calamity with the
sea monkeys, I noticed another advert in the pages of *Look-in*
on how to become a muscle man like a certain Charles Atlas
in America. Everything in America was bigger. Mr Atlas
had more impressive muscles than the Incredible Hulk, and
it said in the advert that if I bought his book and got big
muscles like him, then no bullies would ever kick sand in
my face again. I couldn't remember anyone ever kicking
sand in my face in Millisle – not even a skinhead – because
the sand was always too wet and heavy with the rain, but
I did like the idea of becoming a big strong muscle man,
like this Charles Atlas in America. It would make me safer
from robbers on a Friday night and would certainly help if
the Provos really did decide to make paperboys 'legitimate
targets'. I would be able to lift a dozen paperbags in one
hand and Titch McCracken in the other. I would be strong
enough to lift Oul' Mac's van over the barricades in slow
motion, like the Six Million Dollar Man himself.

It took a long time to receive a response after I sent off
my 50p postal order, but I knew Charles lived in America
and realised that it would take a while for him to get back to
me. However, on the morning the reply eventually arrived,
I was once again disappointed. I spotted the envelope in the
hall, shortly after the postman called: it was sticking out
from underneath a flier about a sale in the Great Universal

Club Book. I retrieved this long-awaited passport to power immediately.

Aware of the slagging potential this delivery could provide for my big brother, I headed straight for my bedroom to open the package in private. When I ripped open the envelope with my feeble arms, instead of a book telling me how to get muscles, I was greeted by a pile of leaflets explaining that I needed to send off another, much larger, postal order to buy the book telling me how to get bigger muscles. Then, as luck would have it, before I could stuff the information pack into the bin, my big brother walked into my room. Catching sight of the incriminating documents, he grabbed them, quickly scanned them and began to laugh. He seemed unable to stop laughing, in fact, and this attracted my mother into my bedroom, too. When she arrived, Mammy lifted up the pack and then began to laugh too. Finally, hearing all the hilarity from downstairs, my father and wee brother joined us and before very long, there they all were in my bedroom: my whole family, laughing hysterically like the Martian robots on the Smash advert on the TV. Not even the thick woodchip on my bedroom walls could absorb the sound of their hysterical laughter.

There was one short gap in the guffaws, when my mother asked breathlessly, 'Is anyone kicking sand in your face at the caravan, love? Cos your Daddy'll deal with them, so he will!' Then, before I could even attempt to answer, the laughter recommenced with added vigour. Charles Atlas went straight into the Parkray fire. The bin wasn't good enough to assuage my anger and humiliation.

My most successful purchase from an advert at the

back of *Look-in* was a pen pal. It said I could choose which country I preferred my pen pal to come from and whether I preferred a boy or a girl. My preferences were for a girl from Sweden or America who liked music – but I got a pen pal called Winston from New Zealand who played rugby. For a while, however, we enjoyed writing to each other.

I was sure Winston must have been disappointed about getting a male pen pal from Northern Ireland because he had probably wanted a girl from Sweden too, but he turned out to be very interested in the Troubles. He was always kind enough to ask at the end of every letter if the British had killed anyone in my family since his last letter. He also assured me of his full support for my people in fighting for freedom from the British invaders. I never responded – in the same way that he never replied to my question as to whether he had a pet kangaroo. I wrote long letters about what I did at school on airmail paper which was even thinner than a page of the *Belfast Telegraph*, and when Winston replied, I was able to add his New Zealand stamps to my growing collection. We corresponded for over a year. Once he realised that we had televisions in Ireland too, we discovered that we both watched *Doctor Who*. However, the letters ceased shortly after I asked him if there was a Bay City Rollers fan club in New Zealand.

But I wasn't going to let a minor discouragement like this dampen my own enthusiasm for the Rollers. Since hearing about their forthcoming trip to Belfast from Pammy Wynette, I had been saving every spare tip in anticipation of the moment the tickets for the concert in the Ulster Hall finally went on sale in Spin-a-Disc. When that feted day arrived, the queue went right around the block: it was longer than the daily queues for water during the Ulster Workers' strike when the men at the Water Board had cut off our water to keep us British. Along with half the teenagers of the Shankill, I waited for hours and finally emerged triumphant from Spin-a-Disc, clutching my very own ticket to go and see Woody, Eric, Alan, Leslie and Derek performing live in the Ulster Hall. There was a massive Bay City Rollers fan base in Belfast. We did tartan exceptionally well.

Our whole gang got tickets for that concert. There was me and my big brother, Heather Mateer, who was the oldest and looked after the money for the tickets, her friend Lynn McQuiston with the buck teeth, former paperboy Titch McCracken, Irene Maxwell, who was still in love with Big Jaunty, Sharon Burgess, who was now, as I have said, my official girlfriend, and Philip Ferris, another paperboy, who said the Rollers were 'ballicks' but wanted to go and see them anyway.

Philip, whose da had coached the Boys' Brigade football team to victory in 1975, was always very hard to impress. He said a lot of things were 'ballicks' – even being a paperboy for Oul' Mac. This seemed very ungrateful to me. At the Westy Disco, every time any song came on that Philip didn't like, he just said 'ballicks' and walked off to the tuck shop. This happened quite a lot. You would be up on the dance floor doing the Slush to Elton John and Kiki Dee and then the Osmonds would come on. Then, from behind, you would hear Philip Ferris shouting 'ballicks', before heading off for a packet of Tayto Cheese & Onion. He seemed unworthy of a Bay City Rollers ticket, really. And ours were no ordinary tickets either: we had got the last balcony tickets. I had never sat in a balcony before.

The next day, I brought my treasured ticket into BRA to show it off, but I was surprised and disappointed at the lack of enthusiasm in the playground. Tartan was clearly less popular at grammar school. Not everyone was impressed, and they weren't just pretending to be not impressed because they were jealous, like when you came top of the class in English. My former fellow band member, Ian from the TITS, just shook his head, told me to 'wise a bap' and slapped me across the head with his *NME*. I didn't tell the teacher on him, in case I got my ticket confiscated along with Ian's *NME*. I just couldn't understand this hostility. I accepted the Rollers weren't a serious rock band like Status Quo, but they were always No.1 on *Top of the Pops*, and they were brilliant to sing along to in the Westy Disco and on Downtown Radio.

When I told Mr Rowing at my next guitar lesson that I was going to see the Bay City Rollers, he just said 'Lovely!', and redirected me back to Tom Dooley. He clearly had no idea who they were!

Nevertheless, I once again refused to be put off by this lack of appreciation of my musical tastes. I had never been to see a real pop concert before. I had once won a ticket in a raffle to go and see *The Wombles* at the ABC in Belfast, but that was cancelled after the first night because everyone complained it was just men dressed up in suits: it was even on the news headlines before the bombs that day. Most of the big pop stars didn't do concerts in Belfast, of course, because they thought we would kill them. Cliff Richard came over every year to do a gospel concert — but that was always on his own with an acoustic guitar, because his band was too scared to come with him. Cliff must have believed God would keep him safe from us. But hardly anyone else ever came, so the Bay City Rollers playing in Belfast was a really big deal to the legions of parallel-trousered and tartan-scarved youths. After all, we had had tartan gangs on the Shankill long before the Bay City Rollers ever existed.

I kept my ticket safely hidden beneath my remote-controlled Dalek in my room, waiting patiently for the months to pass until I could exchange it for an audience with the Scottish gods of rock in the historic surroundings of the Ulster Hall in Belfast city centre. This ticket would be my wisest financial investment of that time. It was worth every routed robber, every hailstone soaking and every slither on Petra's poop. I had earned it, so I had.

# CHAPTER EIGHT

## *good livin'*

I got saved on a bin at the caravan, so I did. Uncle John, the Good News Club leader, said I had put my sin in the bin. I felt very clean on the inside, even though I was never very clean on the outside at the caravan. The only time I came into contact with water there was whenever we took a paddle in the Irish Sea on the days the sun came out. There was an electric shower at the caravan site that took 50p coins for ten minutes of hot water, but there was always a queue, and I preferred to keep my 50ps for the dodgems at the amusement arcade.

The caravan site we went to every summer was in Ballywhiskin, on the outskirts of the County Down seaside resort of Millisle. It was also known as 'Shankill-on-Sea', because the whole Road went there for the Twelfth Fortnight – and our family was no exception. If the Shankill was the heartland of Loyalist Ulster, then Millisle was the Loyalist Riviera. The atmosphere was different beside the sea, though. Even though it was July and the middle of marching season, the Tartan gangs never looked as tough in Millisle, somehow. When they took off their Rangers tops and licked 99s in the sunshine, they looked too soft, white and skinny for kicking your head in. As you strolled along the seafront, even the skinheads shouting, 'Who the f**k are you lookin' at?' in the sunlight seemed less intimidating when they were simultaneously tackling a pink candy floss.

My parents had bought a second-hand caravan on hire purchase at the start of the Troubles. It was a major financial commitment. Only a lot of overtime at the foundry and a lot of sewing for posh ladies made it happen. The said caravan was a static on four legs – not a touring model like rich people with tweed car coats in England had. It was a Pemberton: that means it was rather plush. Adding the word 'Pemberton' before caravan was a bit like adding the word 'respray' after Ford Escort. It meant you were a cut above the rest of your street. My mother always said the word 'Pemberton' quite loudly when talking to anyone about our caravan while in the Post Office queue. This was something to shout about.

The Pemberton had mustard upholstery, a gas grill where I singed my eyebrows toasting Veda, and an amazing pull-down bed, which your grandparents could sleep on if they came down for the weekend and got too drunk, and embarrassed your parents in a pub in Millisle and then slept for a long time, while your father vowed 'never again!'

The best place in the caravan, however, was the bedroom I shared with my big brother. It had bunk beds – the most exciting of all beds – with our own little window to look out at the dump next door to the caravan site. My big brother let me have the top bunk, on the unspoken understanding that this did not imply in any way that he was not top dog in any other circumstance. I loved the reassuring sound of summer rain dancing on the caravan roof when I was tucked up in my bunk bed after a long day of one-armed bandits, fish suppers and beachcombing. For me, it was the most comforting drumming sound of summer.

We had many happy times in our wee tin box in the rain in a field, so we did. From the main windows, you had a lovely view of the beach and the sea beyond the dump. Some of the parents were constantly complaining, saying that the dump should be filled in, but the kids enjoyed catapulting the rats and playing in the old car that rested there, year in, year out. We shared our field beside the dump with twenty other families in caravans of all shapes and sizes. They weren't all from the Shankill. Some of our caravan neighbours – including Big Ruby who taught me how to kiss properly, in the sand dunes – were from exotic places I had never been to, like the Newtownards Road.

The 1969 Pemberton was mainly our holiday home, but my father made it clear that it was always there if we ever needed to get out of Belfast in a hurry. It was reassuring to know that if we got burnt out at least we had somewhere good to go. I had dreams of being a refugee in Millisle, driven from my home by the IRA in balaclavas and exiled to a life of dodgems and dulse on the County Down coast. But things never got bad enough, and by the time my brother and I were paperboys, the caravan was beginning to lose its attraction. We had work to do: paper money to collect on Fridays and *Ulsters* to deliver on Saturdays. Millisle wasn't within the commuter belt for paperboys.

I was eight when I asked Jesus into my heart on the bin at the caravan. The Good News Club was a 'wee meetin'' for children every day for a week in July. There the aunts and uncles, volunteers from the Baptist Church in Newry, would encourage us to get saved. Every day all the kids emptied out of the caravans to go to the Good News Club. It was brilliant fun, especially if you had already lost all your pocket money in the slot machines in Millisle, read your *Whizzer and Chips* Summer Special five times and were bored with trying to find live crabs in the rock pools at the beach. We played games and bible quizzes and won pencils and rubbers and rulers with John 3:16 on them. We sang wee choruses about Jesus with guitars. An aunt or an uncle would hold up a big book with the words of the song on it, and this usually had illustrations of boys and girls and crosses.

One of my favourite choruses was a song called 'Good News'. For this one, the songbook had pictures of a paperboy with cap and an armful of newspapers and, when it came to the last line, we had to shout out the word 'Extra!' like a paperboy shouting in the street. I confess I sometimes got distracted from the Good News itself, because I was too busy imagining that one day I would be a paperboy shouting 'Extra!' around the streets of Belfast. Little did I know then my dream would come true in just a few short years.

The aunts and uncles were very young and happy, for religious people, and thankfully my father noticed this, and I was allowed to go to the wee meetin's. Dad was an atheist, though my mother was Presbyterian. He said religion was 'all superstitious twaddle', but he had agreed that his children could be christened in the Presbyterian Church because my mother was a believer, and just in case it would be bad luck not to get us done. At grammar school, I would meet a few more atheists – David Pritchard, for example, who told me he had stopped believing in God because his father had died. He said religion was a crutch for weak people. My father's father was also dead, so I wondered if God only existed when He kept your father alive.

Atheists at Belfast Royal Academy were not uncommon, but it was quite unusual to be a non-believer on the Shankill. All the murals on the gable walls said we were 'For God and Ulster' – although I noticed most people were really much more for Ulster than for God. So, while I was allowed to go to Sunday school, I was generally forbidden from going to any 'wee meetin's' where my father thought I might be 'brainwashed by the born-agains'. However, he had noticed that the aunts and uncles at the Good News Club were young and very friendly compared to the gospel-tract distributors at home, and he was surprised to see the women were actually allowed to wear jeans, so he relaxed the rules at the caravan.

Even though I was allowed to go to the wee meetin's, I was aware of Dad's concerns that I could be brainwashed, which I knew was what they sometimes did to people in James Bond movies, but no one at the Good News Club was from Russia or ever locked me in a room strapped to a chair in the dark to force me to get born again. Instead, the aunts and uncles, in their jeans, told us stories from the Bible and the amazing adventures of heroic missionaries saving the natives in Africa and China. We sang choruses about Jesus taking all our sin away, and for a while I forgot about Belfast and barricades and the Eleven Plus and everything. We sat on a huge blanket on the grass on sunny days, but when it was rainy, we met inside a small caravan or in the bungalow at the entrance to the caravan site where the owner stored the new bins. These shiny aluminium bins became sacred. They were our pews.

It was in the summer of 1972 that I got saved, the same year as Bloody Friday in Belfast, when the bloody Munich Olympics were on TV, and bloody Donny Osmond was at No.1 with 'Puppy Love'. I was jealous of Donny because all the girls fancied him. However, I had always liked Jesus at Sunday school. He seemed kinder than God and more human than Donny. God was definitely a good, sound Ulster Protestant, but He was always wagging his finger at me like a grumpy old Orangeman.

God was like a big cosmic Paisley, only not as popular in our street. On the other hand, Jesus, according to the wee choruses we sang in Sunday school, loved me, 'this I know, for the Bible tells me so'. He even loved me in the King James version. God locked up the swings in Woodvale Park on a Sunday, but Jesus loved 'all the little children of the world'. It occurred to me that if He did indeed love 'red and yellow, black and white', and that if all were really 'precious in His sight', then He might even love the Green the same as the Orange! Maybe Catholics and Protestants were no more different than the *Radio Times* and the *TV Times*: alternative formats – one a bit heavier than the other – but basically the same content. I kept this heresy to myself, though. I knew it was unlikely to win me a prize in Ballygomartin Presbyterian Church on Children's Day.

Sitting on the bin at the caravan site that summer day in 1972, it had all seemed so simple. I did bad stuff, Jesus wanted to wash it all away, so I asked him to. But even when

I got back to our caravan that day and talked about my spiritual encounter, I discovered there was so much more to it. Granda paused from a sip of stout to say I had been 'led up the garden path'. I wasn't sure what that meant, but it made me feel stupid. Next, Dad expressed concerns I couldn't quite grasp: something about 'no son of mine being brainwashed by no born-again bigots'. It seemed a born-again son was an atheist father's worst nightmare. Worst of all, Granny then started to cry, and said it was tears of joy, like when Paisley got elected. She said she thought it was lovely that I had become a 'wee good livin' boy', that maybe one day I would become a minister – and then she added cryptically, 'especially with him and his bad heart and all!'

Although upset, I knew I must humbly absorb all of these remarks, as a martyr to my new-found faith. If the missionaries in the stories at the Good News Club got beaten and eaten, then I should be able to cope with these persecutions. I prayed sincerely that all of them too would be saved and also that this bad heart of mine – now with Jesus in it – would keep on beating.

When I returned home from Millisle, I soon learned the full truth about the whole religious package I had so spontaneously embraced. The burden of it all soon became heavier than a paperbag when you had thirty extra *Tellys* to carry because one of the other paperboys was off to the clinic with nits.

For a start, the Shankill was coming down with churches. There were even more churches than pubs. If you fell out with the minister in one church – as lots of people did – you could always join, or even start, another church in the next street. Lots of old men in church always talked about how in the 1859 Revival, everyone had got saved in tents. They said we should all pray for it to happen again, but it never did. Maybe God was fed up with us being more for Ulster than for Him, because the more they prayed for revival, the more people I knew stopped going to church.

I remember how one Sunday – it was during the first year of my paper-delivery days – when Reverend Lowe, our regular minister, was on holiday, we had a visiting minister with a turn in his eye. This man took it upon himself to explain to us the difference between all the churches.

'The Presbyterian Church is as near as humanly possible to the Church on earth that God intended,' he announced.

I was shocked by this, because in our church, the roof was leaking and the organ kept breaking down. I searched the visiting minister's face for an impish smile, but such an expression was clearly a stranger to his visage. He was serious! I knew Protestants were God's chosen people, but I didn't think Presbyterians were perfect, and our church certainly wasn't. The church bells blasted out from a cassette tape recorder plugged into big speakers in the bell tower every Sunday morning, because we couldn't afford real bells, which no one would have known how to ring anyway. One Sunday morning, someone put on the wrong tape, and instead of church bells chiming out, we had had Philomena Begley singing 'One Day at a Time' – and she was a Catholic!

Titch McCracken's cousin from Ballymoney had told me when he was down visiting that Ulster Protestants were the last descendants of the 'Lost Tribe of Israel'. He was very convincing, but when I looked up Israel in my geography atlas, I concluded that either Titch's cousin was wrong or we were a very lost tribe indeed.

Having established that we were the champions as far as religion went, the visiting minister then turned his attention to the other churches. The most obvious target was first.

'The Roman Catholic Church is corrupt and evil, and its misguided adherents are doomed to hellfire and damnation!' he declared.

That always went down well on the Shankill. This man knew how to get his audience on side.

'Its Pope is the Antichrist!'

Now, I had heard this one before, but I always thought the Pope looked like quite a nice man, and when I stared very closely at him on *John Craven's Newsround*, I could never make out a 666 on his forehead. Anyway, the Antichrist was Damien in *The Omen*.

'The Church of Ireland is so close to the Church of Rome as to be indistinguishable. It is not a Christian church, and its people are in error,' the minister continued.

I was shocked again. My guitar teacher, Mr Rowing, and his wife were Church of Ireland, and they seemed so much kinder than this man, and, as far as I was concerned, Mr Rowing's only error was not to teach me 'Mull of Kintyre'.

'The Methodists have departed from the truth to serve a social gospel,' he pontificated.

I think that meant they help poor people. Now I was getting angry. Reverend Lowe never made me angry like this. The Methodists at the Grosvenor Hall had taken my mother on holidays to Bangor when she was a poor wee girl with nothing.

'They neglect the sinner's need to make Jesus their own and personal Saviour,' he elaborated.

My pompous preacher friend next went on to explain that we should not waste money by sending food to Africans because we needed to send missionaries to get them saved first, as that was more important. I couldn't work out how you could give them salvation if they had already died of starvation.

Then he turned his eye on the smaller denominations.

'The Baptists and Pentecostals and all the rest are nothing but little tin-hut Christians,' he said.

He didn't even cite a verse from the Bible to back this one up. This final condemnation was the most confusing of all, because I knew from listening to Mrs Piper in our street and from some of my friends in school that Baptists thought Presbyterians weren't Christians, and Brethren and Pentecostals said we weren't saved either.

Leaving the church that Sunday morning, I tried to avoid eye contact with this man as he shook hands at the door, but his errant eye seemed to follow me nonetheless.

On the Shankill, a 'good livin'' person was someone who had put their hand up to get saved at a gospel meeting (otherwise known as a 'wee meetin'). This usually happened at the end of the wee meetin'. For about half an hour the preacher asked you to raise your hand if you wanted to be saved, while the organist played fifteen verses of the hymn, 'Just as I Am'. That usually gave you enough time.

Some people I knew got saved every week. They got born again, again and again. Once you were saved, you didn't curse or drink or smoke or go to the cinema or discos. If you had done any of these sins a lot before you were saved, you got asked to give your testimony at wee meetin's, and you stood up and told everyone all the worst sins you had ever committed in great detail. The biggest sinners were the best.

I found all of this spiritually perplexing. The list of what you weren't allowed to do got longer every day. You weren't allowed to watch TV on a Sunday or buy a raffle ticket, even for an African baby! Of course it was worse for girls: they had lots of extras they weren't allowed to do, like wear trousers, or speak. I was baffled. I thought it was all supposed to have something to do with Jesus.

But soon after my road to Damascus moment on the bin in Millisle, neighbours and relatives, when trying to distinguish me from my two brothers, started referring to me as the 'wee good livin' one'. My older brother had put his hand up at a meeting once and got saved, but he said 'f**k' twice the next day and so gave it up. And my wee brother was still too young to put his hand up at all. The only thing worse than being called 'good livin'' was that you were always described as 'wee'. You couldn't just be a 'good livin' fella' – you had to be a 'wee good livin' boy'. At a certain point, I was taller than both my brothers, but I was the one that was being called 'wee'!

I faithfully attended and remained true to the principles of the Good News Club until well into my time as a paperboy. And so Mrs Mac always called me a 'wee good

livin' boy' too. I put up with it, because I just knew I was
her favourite paperboy. Good livin' meant no thievin' in
her books, and she kept Oul' Mac's accounts right to the
last halfpenny. Mrs Mac was a tough old Belfast woman,
like my granny: a bit scary, but with a warm heart. She
didn't curse quite as much as Oul' Mac but she could give
him a good run for his money, if Mrs Beattie from No.
21 complained about you leaving her gate open or letting
her Jack Russell out or giving her cheek after she'd called
you 'a lazy wee skitter'.

   Mrs Mac was quite glamorous for her age. She used
a jewelled cigarette holder like an American woman in
the black-and-white movies, so she didn't have yellow
fingers like Oul' Mac. Her hands were elegant even
when they were black with newspapers, and she had
fancy handwriting when she wrote the addresses on the
magazines. She looked like one of those old film-star
actresses interviewed on *Parkinson* on a Saturday night,
who looked better in black and white, and too pink on
colour TV. Mrs Mac had red painted nails and big gold
rings on nearly all of her fingers. This was evidence of
what some of the other paperboys used to say about the
Macs. 'Them uns is loaded', they would say. But I couldn't
see how selling newspapers could make you all that rich.
Perhaps they had won 'Spot the Ball' in one of their
millions of *Belfast Telegraphs*. Mrs Mac had a beehive too,
which, my mother told me, was all the rage in the sixties.
I knew this was true because Cilla Black and Petula Clark
had beehives on the old LP covers in our stereogram in
the sitting room.

One Eleventh Night I had to leave the paper money round to the Macs' house as the shop was already closed for the Twelfth. When she came to the door, Mrs Mac was in a wonderful mood. She was winking at Oul' Mac and laughing a lot, and she seemed a little more unsteady on her feet than usual.

'Thanks love,' she said, taking the bag full of warm and fragrant coins, fresh from my Doc Martens. As I was leaving her house with my burdens lightened, carefully closing her gate tight after me, she called out to me, 'Enjoy yourself at the boney the night, son! That's a good boy.'

As I turned to thank her, I am sure I heard a muted fart, and a lock of long hair fell forlornly out of the beehive across her tortoise-shell glasses. I'd never heard a lady fart before.

The day after the Showaddywaddy guy had put a gun in my back, my father brought me round to the Macs' house to explain the whole drama. Their house was full of gold-framed mirrors, copper bubble wallpaper and china dogs on every available window sill. There was not a newspaper in sight.

When he heard about the Showaddywaddy guy, Oul' Mac was so furious I thought he was going to spit out one of his looser teeth, but poor Mrs Mac was just very shocked and concerned. She gave me a big hug, looked at my father with tears welling up in her eyes and then, cocking her head to one side, she said, 'And him a wee good livin' boy, too.'

# CHAPTER NINE

## *wider horizons*

I was not well travelled, so I wasn't. I had left Ireland only once in my life, on a primary-school trip to Ayr in Scotland. But the experience was marred when the teacher slapped me around the head because I had been ungrateful enough to fall asleep in the cinema during the *On the Buses* movie. So I got homesick and hated that teacher ever after.

However, as I thumbed through my *Belfast Telegraphs* night after night, I discovered unexpected information within those pages that fuelled a new desire to see the wider world. It was the holiday section that always caught my eye. There were ads for a week in a caravan in Donegal, where my father had climbed up on the roof of the toilets to rescue my kite, but we stopped going there when the Troubles started in case it helped bring a United Ireland. Donegal always confused me because everyone said it was down south but on the map in my geography class it was further north than most of the North. Nobody seemed to notice. Maybe compasses were different in Donegal.

Then I discovered that at the back of the *TV Times* there were adverts for trips to more faraway places, like the Isle of Man and Blackpool and the Costa Brava, where Judith Chalmers got a tan every week on UTV. The more I devoured the holiday ads in the newspapers and magazines my profession brought me into contact with, the more I longed to travel to these long-haul destinations.

I had always enjoyed the caravan and the candy floss in Millisle, but I began to dream of wider horizons, so I did. I wanted to go to Sweden, where ABBA lived on an island with a piano and snow and fur coats. I wanted to visit London, where they made *Top of the Pops* and Wimpy burgers and the Royal Family lived. I longed to go to Italy to see where a volcano in my history book had buried everyone, even the dogs. I wanted to visit China, where they had a huge wall you could see from outer space. Apparently it was bigger than the peace wall between the Falls and the Shankill – and they didn't even have Protestants and Catholics in China! As I dutifully delivered my daily papers on automatic pilot, I daydreamed of flying on a jet plane to America, where they made big cars and movies and Osmonds. I would also imagine myself on a trek across Australia, where Skippy the Bush Kangaroo would be there to save me if I ever fell down a disused mine shaft. Of course, I also had dreams of travelling to the planet Vulcan, but there were never any package deals to that particular destination advertised in the *Belfast Telegraph*.

Unfortunately, I knew rightly that not even the pooled resources of my father's overtime earnings at the foundry, my mother's income from extra sewing for swanky ladies up the Lisburn Road, my big brother's poker winnings in the garden shed and several bootfuls of my Christmas tips would ever be enough to finance any trips to these exotic destinations. I envied boys in my class like Timothy

Longsley, whose parents said all their 'ings' and were always go-ing holiday-ing to their cottage in eff-ing France.

But then fate intervened in my favour, in the way that it sometimes did – like those times I would unexpectedly bump into Sharon Burgess in Woodvale Park in her hot pants. For, all of a sudden, it seemed that everybody wanted to send us poor kids from the Shankill on trips away from the Troubles. It was amazing! The nice people with all the money for trips must have heard that the Westy Disco was full of poor wee potential petrol-bombers, who needed taken away from war-torn Belfast. And so, suddenly and unexpectedly, exciting new opportunities for travel began to open up for us. And as we were wee deprived children from West Belfast, the trips were absolutely free: we didn't have to pay a single penny, which meant more spending money for buying sweetie mice to eat on the journey. Yes, these trips were as free as a Captain Scarlet badge in a box of Sugar Puffs. The only problem for me was recruiting a sufficiently trustworthy substitute paperboy to stand in for me while I was away. But I could be quite resourceful when I needed to be.

My first free trip was up to Corrymeela. This was in Ballycastle, County Antrim, beside the sea, where you got 'yellowman' honeycomb that stuck in your teeth, and dulse that made you sick on your parallels in the minibus on the way home. A man with a beard had phoned Auntie Emma from the Westy Disco to ask us to come to Corrymeela to get away from the riots for a day, so Uncle Henry organised three free handicapped minibuses for the trip.

We weren't allowed to sing 'The Sash' or smoke as they transported us up the coast to Ballycastle. En route, I noticed that the County Antrim coast had more cliffs and fewer skinheads than the County Down coast I knew so well. Corrymeela itself was a big white wooden house on a cliff where they liked peace and wore Aran jumpers. I liked peace too, because I was the only pacifist paperboy in West Belfast, but I wasn't so keen on the knitwear. They mustn't have had a John Frazer's in Ballycastle.

As soon as we arrived at Corrymeela, the whole thirty of us spilled out of the three handicapped minibuses and jumped onto a seesaw and broke it. Auntie Emma was scundered, and the man in an Aran jumper who was about to welcome us in an English accent looked quite scared. We were wilder than the waves in the sea below the cliffs. Then we played brilliant games – organised by men with beards – on a big field, and afterwards we got free juice and biscuits served by smiling ladies with rainbow scarves. It was the best fun ever. I loved it. Nearly everybody loved it. Peace was free. Peace was fun! Even my big brother said it was 'class'. Lynn McQuiston with the buck teeth said it was 'weeker', but Titch McCracken said half the men with beards were Catholics called Brendan, and, somewhat predictably, Philip Ferris said it was 'ballicks'.

After we had our free juice and biscuits, we were handed out song sheets, and then one of the bearded Brendans started to play the guitar and got us to join in a singalong on a blanket on the ground at the top of the cliff. We sang 'Puff the Magic Dragon', 'Lord of the Dance' and 'Kumbaya'. We may have been wee deprived kids from up the Shankill, but when we stopped messin' and started singing the same song at the same time (and when Titch McCracken stopped shouting 'Kick the Pope!' between verses), we actually began to sound quite good. It was as 'Someone's singing Lord, Kumbaya' drifted out over the cliff edge towards Rathlin Island that Uncle Henry had his most inspired idea since introducing the breathalyser at the door into the Westy Disco.

'Let's start a youth-club choir!' he suddenly proposed.

'Aye! Dead on!' shouted wee Sandra Hull, through her snatter tracks. Sharon Burgess smiled and nodded shyly. Heather Mateer cheered, jumping up so quickly that she split her parallels and we saw her knickers, and giggled inappropriately the whole way through 'Someone's crying Lord, Kumbaya'. Most of the girls thought the choir was a wonderful idea and squealed with excitement. The seagulls above us joined in a screeching chorus of noisy agreement. The boys were a little more restrained in their enthusiasm, because boys didn't sing and choirs were for homos.

'Wise-ick!' said my big brother.

'Ballicks,' said Philip Ferris.

'Sure, give it a go, lads,' requested Uncle Henry.

We trusted him, so we did. We would give it a go! We spent the rest of the day talking excitedly about the new musical vistas now opening up before us. Uncle Henry was in a brilliant mood and didn't even get too angry when we left Corrymeela to visit the scenic harbour nearby, and Titch McCracken broke into a digger and tried to drive it into the sea. We were escorted from Ballycastle by the RUC.

The scene was set. We were to form the first Upper Shankill youth-club choir. We would practise every Tuesday night after I had done the papers and tortuous trigonometry homework. The next time we would be taken on a free trip, it wouldn't be just as poor wee troublemakers from West Belfast. We would be travelling by special invitation, as a performing choir on tour. All of this meant yet more opportunities to broaden my horizons, of course.

When the booking for our first international gig came in, the venue was perfect. We received an invitation to sing in the very birthplace of Rollermania, the land of the Mull of Kintyre itself. Yes, our first overseas performance was to be in Scotland, across the water on the Larne–Stranraer ferry. For years, we had revelled in the music that Scotland had brought to us through Woody, Eric, Alan, Leslie and Derek: now it was our turn to return the favour. We were going to bring the music back to Scotland! Patrick Walsh at the School of Music said all Protestants should go back to Scotland anyway.

Our debut destination was Edinburgh; we were invited to sing at St Philip's Church in the city. It was a Church of Scotland church, which I thought was just Church of Ireland with a Scottish accent, but it turned out that the Church of Scotland was Presbyterian like us, except with fewer flags. Presbyterians were official in Scotland, it seemed. We would be spending a week seeing the sights of Edinburgh and then sing at the church service on the Sunday morning before getting the boat back home. I was determined to go, so I arranged for the wee ginger boy with National Health glasses that I bullied to do my paper round for the week. In a momentary lapse from my pacifist principles, I threatened to kick his teeth in if he stole any of the paper money. In the words of our Reverend Lowe, it was, as far as I was concerned, the lesser of two evils.

After months of saving, I had at last been able to buy my very own Harrington jacket – complete with tartan lining – and I wore it proudly on the day of the journey to Scotland. 'That's a quare nice new Harrington you've got, wee lad,' observed Irene Maxwell, as we boarded the boat. Irene knew everything about fashion, from *Jackie* magazine.

The Larne–Stranraer ferry smelt of salt and fish and vomit, and it made me feel very queasy. While most of my fellow choristers were enjoying a pastie supper in the canteen below decks, and some were secretly sampling vodka and coke in the bar, I ended up spending most of the voyage up on deck in the fresh air, in a desperate attempt to keep down the tomato sandwiches my mother had made me for the journey. I tried to distract myself from the feelings of nausea by pretending I was James Bond, working undercover on a cruiser in the Caribbean, wearing a white suit and trying to catch a diamond thief, but eventually the tomato sandwiches defied gravity and returned. As the contents from my stomach spewed over the side of the Larne–Stranraer ferry, an insulting wind from the surface of the Irish Sea blew my boke back on me. My prized Harrington jacket smelled rotten for weeks.

'Are you calling for Hughey and you're not even in Scotland yet?' enquired my big brother sympathetically, as he passed me on the deck while I was in mid-vomit.

When at last we arrived on dry land and travelled up to Edinburgh, I was completely awestruck. I had never seen a city like this before, apart from on *Blue Peter*. There was a big castle on a hill and a toy museum and huge shops, where they didn't search you to get in. I kept raising my arms automatically to any adult standing at the entrance doors of these shops, until people looked at me strangely and I realised that you weren't searched for bombs on the way into shops over here.

In Princes Street, there was a clock made of flowers, and shops selling nothing but tartan. Here I found the real Macaulay tartan that you couldn't get in John Frazer's in Belfast and bought a strip for my mother to sew down the side of my parallels for the much-anticipated Bay City Rollers concert. Most exciting of all were the real old-fashioned blue police telephone boxes, which, when no one was looking, I pretended were my TARDIS. Every day at one o'clock, the big cannons fired from the top of the castle. The whole youth-club choir jumped in unison every time this happened, because we thought it was a car bomb.

We had been practising for months for this premiere performance. The Scottish Presbyterians had heard we were very good in spite of all our sufferings, and I could sense that they were looking forward to our Sunday show with great anticipation. However, as the week went by, I began to feel a little nervous: I wondered if their expectations might be a little too high. I feared they might be disappointed. I knew we could sing okay, and our performances always went down very well on Children's Day in Ballygomartin Presbyterian Church, but the youth-club choir wasn't like the choir at

BRA. At school, we read the musical score, and the teacher used a baton, making funny faces like a real conductor. In the youth-club choir, we had no music to follow — only the words copied out on carbon paper — and Uncle Henry just waved his hands encouragingly and counted us in at the right time. At home, everyone thought we were the best choir ever, because we were singing instead of fighting, but in Scotland maybe they would have higher expectations.

We had three pieces to perform that Sunday morning: our three best ones. They were 'When a Child is Born', 'This Little Light of Mine' and 'Any Dream Will Do.' We sang 'When a Child is Born' all year round, and not just at Christmas like Johnny Mathis. This was the only song we sang that had been on *Top of the Pops*, so we knew it was cool. The recital in Edinburgh began with this anthem. We started off a little nervously, but soon got into our stride: Johnny Mathis would have been proud of us. We were standing on a raised stage at the front of the church. When it came to the spoken part, and Heather Mateer said, in her best American accent, the bit about turning tears into laughter, hate into love, war into peace and everyone into each other's neighbour, I could see two old Scottish women in hats in the front row getting their hankies out. They loved us! We were a symbol of hope in a violent and cruel world.

In the next song, I was to play a starring role. It was 'This Little Light of Mine', a fast country-and-western gospel song that didn't work with an organ accompaniment, so I was asked to play along on guitar. Thankfully, my Spanish guitar had sustained no further damage on the boat journey and so I was all set. I was nervous about the important role

I had to play, but I was fairly confident too, because the song had the same two chords as 'Tom Dooley', and I had practised it to death. Mr Rowing would have been proud of me, playing guitar up on stage on tour in another country. I was sure that Paul McCartney's guitar teacher must have felt similar pride the first time he heard Paul performing in public.

I strummed 'This Little Light of Mine' with all my heart and determination, and the choir kept up admirably. A man at the back of the church started to clap his hands in time with the rhythm. If this had happened at home, a fat lady with a tweed beret would have turned around and shushed him, and he would have had to stop. But clapping wasn't a sin in the Church of Scotland, it seemed.

It was all going very well until we came to the final verse, when we cleverly adapted the lyrics: 'Shine all over Scotland, I'm gonna let it shine.' In the excitement, I overdid it, breaking my 'E' string and dropping my plectrum. I had to finish using my thumb, because I had bitten all my nails for a recent Chemistry exam. However, when we finished the song, the whole congregation broke out into a spontaneous applause. I had never heard applause in a church before: I had always thought that God didn't do clapping.

Finally, it was time for our most accomplished work, 'Any Dream Will Do'. It was a song from a musical about Joseph with an amazing Technicolor dreamcoat. There was even a story in the Bible based on it. 'Any Dream Will Do' always got us the biggest applause. The youth-club choir didn't generally do four-part harmony like the school choir, but we could do quite complicated pieces like 'Any Dream

Will Do', where the boys sang the lines 'I closed my eyes', and the girls echoed with an 'Ah-a-ah'. The girls sang their 'Ah-a-ahs' in a Belfast accent. No one could go up at the end of a sentence better than a Belfast girl. Our audiences usually adored this musical intricacy, so we often sang this song as our final piece and as an encore.

We could feel our Scottish audience's sense of expectation grow as our finale drew close. So, when Uncle Henry raised his hands and smiled, getting us ready for the opening bars of the song, there was a hushed atmosphere in the pews of St Philip's. We smiled back in silent harmony: our smiles reflected a quiet assurance that this was going to be good. Uncle Henry counted us in, and then we were off to a harmonious start. Carried away by the music and the atmosphere, I imagined I was Joseph with a Technicolor Harrington jacket and my own pyramid in the desert because, like him, I was a dreamer too. However, disaster was just around the corner, like Oul' Mac's van had been the day he ran over Mrs Grant's pussy.

Nobody else knew that some of the girls, who normally led the 'Ah-a-ahs' so beautifully, had smuggled a bottle of Scottish whisky into the girls' dormitory the night before. Nobody knew they had only managed two hours' sleep. Nobody else knew that they were teetering in the twilight zone between still drunk and hungover. Our fate was sealed.

'I closed my eyes … '

'… I closed my eyes' – It was lovely.

'Pulled back the curtain …'

'… Aaaaaaah huh'

Uncle Henry's smile disappeared as fast as a cat in a hedge being chased by Petra.

'To see for certain …'

'Ugh aaa … Aaaaaaah huh' – It was horrible. The girls began to giggle.

'That was ballicks!' whispered Philip Ferris, much too loudly. The boys began to laugh.

Uncle Henry wasn't laughing. The congregation wasn't laughing. Scotland was not amused. I felt my face go redder and redder. We were rude and disrespectful wee hooligans from Belfast! They had paid for us to come here and sing to them, and we had messed it up with drink as usual! It was humiliating.

I vainly attempted to rescue the next 'Ah-a-ah', but it was too high for me because my voice was breaking. My big brother gave me a dig in the ribs and whispered 'Fruit!' much too loudly.

It was too late. We had fallen apart. 'Any Dream Will Do' had become a nightmare. We had travelled hundreds of miles over land and sea for this performance, and we had fallen on our faces at the last hurdle. The Scottish minister rushed the benediction, bringing the awful embarrassment to a blessed end.

In spite of our collapse, the Scottish Presbyterians were most forgiving: they still cried and gave us big hugs when we were leaving. It was as if we were going back to somewhere terrible, to our certain deaths.

When we finally returned to Belfast after another long journey – which included yet another evacuation of the contents of my stomach into the Irish Sea – I was relieved and glad to be home, so I was. My new Harrington jacket was crumpled and smelly, but I was happy to be back to familiar things, like homework and marbles, army Saracens and my paper round. The eventful trip to Edinburgh had whet my appetite for wider horizons, but it also confirmed to me that no matter what the rest of the world thought about us, there was something I loved about home.

# CHAPTER TEN

## *paper mum*

As a good loyal paperboy, I accepted that Oul' Mac could never be questioned. He was in charge, and so he was always right – even when he was wrong. It was the same with doctors, teachers, paramilitaries, ministers and my granny. All of these were above contradiction. The School of Music was also up there in the same incontestable category. The big bosses there lived near Queen's University, could read music and never dropped a single 'ing' when they were speaking. If they made a decision, it was final.

And so I was presented with a serious dilemma in the second year of my career in Oul' Mac's employ when my School of Music timetable arrived in the post. My new violin-lesson time would clash with my paper round on a Monday night! This was as serious a clash as would ensue in our house when Man United were playing football on BBC 1 at the same time as Elsie Tanner was having an affair on *Coronation Street* on UTV.

The bosses at the School of Music had the power to demote you in the orchestra to an even lower ranking in the second violins. Whereas at Springhill Primary School I had been the leader of the orchestra – the first of the first violins, at the School of Music, I was already languishing so near the back of the second violins that I was almost a third violin. I already had some experience of the humiliation of being a third violin in the BRA school orchestra. This lowly function entailed having to count for twenty bars between short screeches the whole way through a two-hour Gilbert and Sullivan opera, where all the parents with clean hands clapped and laughed at clever jokes by sixth formers acting and singing with English accents. (I preferred Gilbert O'Sullivan anyway.) The big chiefs at the School of Music had in fact so much power that if they were not happy with your performance they could even take your borrowed violin back so that you had to buy a cheap Chinese one that still smelt of smoke from the bomb-damage sale in Crymble's music shop. This would be on a par with Oul' Mac taking your paperbag off you.

The School of Music was across town, in Donegall Pass in South Belfast. This was where my mother had lived in a wee street of terraced houses during the war, except when she was evacuated up the country where Hitler couldn't get her, to live with a posh lady in a big house with a rose garden in Ballykelly. Mammy's old primary school had been turned into the School of Music years ago, and children came to learn music there from all over the city. It was the only school I had ever heard of where Protestants and Catholics were allowed to go together, and nobody ever even tried to stop it.

As far as this present dilemma went, I knew it would be possible to catch a bus from BRA which would take me over to the School of Music in time for my violin lesson there, but I knew I could never get back home again early enough to be able to do my papers, even on a night when the buses weren't being burned. So I was indeed left facing a very difficult choice. This wasn't like my customers choosing between the *TV Times* and the *Radio Times*, or their children deciding between *The Topper* and *The Beano*. No, this was a big decision – like picking your O-Levels or gettin' saved. I would have to choose between my music and my career. I wanted to play the violin like Yehudi Menuhin – or at least get near to the front of the second violins anyway – but I also wanted to have all the benefits of continuous, secure employment with Oul' Mac. It was surely cruel to expect me to choose between the two, but I knew that the violin-lesson timetable was written in stone, and no one would ever dare suggest it be changed.

In spite of all this, I eventually persuaded my mother to ring up the School of Music to try to rearrange the lesson. She was very polite and respectful and used her Gloria Hunniford telephone voice, but there was no question of any change, it seemed, because my new violin teacher was English apparently and 'a very busy man'.

'Told ye, love,' Mammy said, back in her own voice again, as she replaced the receiver, 'You have to learn to fit in with people like that if you want to get on.'

This was without question of course, and so my next problem was my paper round. Who was going to do it? My big brother was the obvious First Division substitute, but he played rugby and sang dirty songs on the minibus up to Mallusk on a Monday, so he was unavailable. My wee brother was still too young to do the papers, because the full bag of *Belfast Telegraphs* was far heavier than him, and he would just have fallen over. Titch McCracken was not an option either, due to the incendiary nature of his relationship with newspapers. The wee ginger boy with National Health glasses that I bullied went to bagpipe lessons in a kilt on a Monday Night. And everyone else I knew was either a girl or already a paperboy or had been sacked at some point by Oul' Mac.

I asked one of my Antrim Road friends from BRA if his father would give him a lift over to do my papers on a Monday night, but his Da said no, because he didn't wanted his Rover being hijacked, he said. I was running out of options. It looked as if I was going to have to choose between two of my most favourite things. It was terrible – like having to choose between *Star Trek* and *Lost in Space*. No, it was worse than that even! It was like having to decide between Olivia Newton-John and Farrah Fawcett-Majors.

Everyone said my mother was a very caring woman, because she was always looking after someone. If she wasn't looking after me and my brothers, she was looking after my father or looking after her father and mother (who took a lot of looking after), or looking after four hundred kids at the Westy Disco on a Saturday night. I sometimes made Mammy a cup of tea with a digestive biscuit, because no one seemed to be looking after her. She was always busy shopping at the Co-op, or sending off cheques to the Great Universal Club Book, or making fish fingers and Smash, or sewing dresses late at night for swanky ladies up the Lisburn Road.

Sometimes when Mammy was having a rest for ten minutes, she invited one of the neighbours like Auntie Emma or Auntie Mabel or Auntie Hetty (who was my real auntie and brought me Lucozade when I was sick) in for a cup of tea and a slice of barmbrack loaf. They would chat about who in our street, apart from Mr Grant of course, was in bed with their chest, who was bad with their nerves and who was looking like mutton dressed as lamb. Often the most animated of these exchanges were concluded with the expression, 'bloody men!'

However, the best parts of these conversations between my mother and her friends were always whispered. I wasn't generally very interested in the noisier chattering, and I sometimes got quite annoyed if they were talking loudly while I was watching John Noakes jumping out of an aeroplane on *Blue Peter*. But when voices were lowered because children were present, I would tune in to listen to the secret stuff.

Sometimes it was all about women's tubes, and I panicked and tuned out again immediately, but on other occasions I gathered fascinating information – such as speculation as to why, if Mrs Piper was that good livin', she had a fancy man from a gospel mission on the Newtownards Road. I also learned that after Trevor Johnston's family had moved to Bangor, his da had been arrested for hijacking a lemonade van for Ulster and was now in prison in the Maze (which was Protestant for Long Kesh).

It was during the time that I was pondering my weighty choice between my career as a paperboy and my future as a virtuoso violinist that, one Saturday afternoon, I found myself privy again to one of these confidential conversations of my mother's. I was to glean a lot of information very pertinent to my situation – and more besides.

Auntie Emma had called in to recommend that my father buy, for that week's upcoming Westy Disco, the new single by Demis Roussos, the big fat Greek man in a dress, which

Uncle Henry said was going to go straight to No.1. She was, however, too late with this sage advice, because, as my mother explained, my da was already on his way to Spin-a-Disc to buy The Wurzels and 'Save Your Kisses for Me' by The Brotherhood of Man. It was clear that the quality of music available around that time was so high that it was proving very hard to choose between singles each week – just like my impossible choice between papers and violin lessons.

'God love our Tony,' my mother was saying. 'The poor wee crater has his violin lesson at the same time as his papers for Oul' Mac, and he can't get any of the other wee lads do them for him. His new violin teacher's English and he wouldn't change it, so he wouldn't, and he's a very busy man, so he is, you know.'

'Och God love him, right enough, Betty,' replied Auntie Emma. 'I don't know, sure your Tony's quare and good at the fiddle and all, but he'd miss his tips at Christmas for buying his stamps, and, sure, Mrs Mac's awful, awful fond of him, so she is.'

I appreciated the sincerity of the sympathy being expressed, but there had been nothing of great import in the conversation, until, that is, Auntie Emma added mysteriously, '... and him with his bad heart and all, the wee crater'.

There it was again. My bad heart. Everyone knew it was bad, except me, it sometimes seemed. How many beats had it left, I wondered? This time I was absolutely determined to find out more, so I helpfully offered to make Mammy and Auntie Emma another cup of tea, so as to give them

space to discuss the matter in private in the living room —
while I listened at the door, instead of buttering barmbrack
in the kitchen, as they thought. I felt like Captain Scarlet
on TV using an electronic listening device to spy on the
Mysterons.

Mammy and Auntie Emma were whispering, but I could
hear every single word.

'What does the doctor say about his wee heart now,
love?' Auntie Emma was asking.

'Well, Mr Pantridge says there's nothing to worry about
and our Tony should do all the same things as a normal boy,
as long as he goes to get it checked up at the Royal every
year,' replied my mother.

I was offended by the suggestion I was not a normal boy,
but I still breathed a huge sigh of relief to hear that, contrary
to all my fears, I was in no imminent danger of a cardiac
arrest. I was going to live! I had a future! I would probably
live long enough to go to Spain and maybe America. And
have sex like Clint Eastwood in the movies and do A-Levels.
And learn to drive and maybe even go to the moon for my
holidays in the year 2000! However, my speculation about
my plans for the rest of my life was interrupted almost
immediately by further revelations.

'It was when he had pneumonia, when he was a wee
baby and we nearly lost him, that done it til his wee heart,'
added my mother.

I dropped the butter knife on the formica kitchen table.
When Mammy said they had nearly lost me, I knew she
wasn't talking about the time I wandered off on my own
into the meat store at the Co-op and the butcher found me

playing in the sawdust. I had, it seemed, nearly died as a baby! This was unbelievable. I had nearly been a tragedy. I almost hadn't lived long enough to pass my Eleven Plus or smell Brut or kiss Sharon Burgess or get a ticket to see the Bay City Rollers!

'Mr Pantridge says lots of people with a heart murmur live normal lives, but that if wee Tony needs to get any teeth out, he has to get them done in the Royal instead of the dentist, just in case,' my mother added, showing off her detailed medical knowledge of my condition to her best pal.

'Och, God love the wee dote,' repeated Auntie Emma.

A few minutes later, as I came in with the fresh cups of tea and buttered barmbrack on a patterned faux-brass tray, Auntie Emma commented:

'You must be freezing, love – your wee hands are shakin', so they are.'

'Och he's a good boy, so he is,' said my mother. 'I'm just going to have to do his papers on a Monday night for him.'

I was shocked. This solution had never even crossed my mind. Girls didn't do papers, never mind mothers! Yet when I thought about it for a while, I knew it was the perfect solution. My mother would never be late and would never nick paper money or give cheek to the pensioners. No wee hoods or robbers from down the Road would dare try to rob a mum, and so she would never need to hide any money down her suede boots.

'Will ye really?' I asked in disbelief.

'Aye, of course I will, love,' Mammy answered warmly. I gave her a big hug, and I didn't even blush when Auntie

Emma felt compelled to offer the sentimental commentary: 'Och God love the wee man, he's all grown up nigh, but he still loves his mammy, so he does.'

And so, every Monday night for three months, my mother delivered forty-eight *Belfast Telegraphs* in the darkness, while her son scratched scales and plucked pathetic *pizzicato* in the same building on the Donegall Road around which she had skipped as a wee girl in the war. She never complained once, even in the hailstones.

Oul' Mac knew about the arrangement and had no complaints either. He already regarded my parents and Auntie Emma and Uncle Henry as near-saints for running the Westy Disco and 'keeping all them cheeky wee shites off the streets on a Saturday night'. Mammy even kept going after Big Aggie, the resident gossip queen of our street, cheekily asked her one Monday night if she was not making enough money from her sewing to look after her kids properly.

It all came to an abrupt end when my new violin teacher refused to teach me any more because I didn't practise enough. In fact, he was to soon stop teaching altogether because he said we were 'all f**king lazy little bastards in this godforsaken country'. Fortunately, I ended up with a nice new violin teacher at a more convenient hour. I took up the reins of my paper round again on Monday nights, and my mother looked relieved: this was one less thing for her to look after.

I never forgot how Mammy saved my job, how she had prevented my career from being needlessly cut short when it had barely begun. I gave her less cheek for months, and a bottle of Charlie perfume for Mother's Day (which was twenty weeks at 10p from the Club Book). Sometimes I even helped her with the dishes, and we laughed when I pretended to be the wee lad in the Fairy Liquid advert, asking her in an English accent, 'Mummy, why are your hands so soft?'

It had not been the first time Mammy had come through for me. And I knew in my heart (which was still a bad heart but nothing to worry about now, unless I had to get any teeth out) that it would not be the last time she would deliver for me either.

# CHAPTER ELEVEN

## *scouts, bombs and bullets*

Every day I was learning about goodies and baddies, so I was. I could soon tell in an instant who were the goodies and who were the baddies. I acquired this skill mainly at home to begin with: my granny, for instance, was brilliant at it. This was an exceptionally good foundation, but I needed to develop greater proficiency still and got ample opportunity to do so on the streets, with the able assistance of the other paperboys. My expertise was then honed by teachers at school, and then blessed by teachers at Sunday school – as often by what they didn't say as by what they did say. Finally, my powers of judgement were perfected by paying attention to the subtext of my favourite television programmes and, of course, to the pages of the *Belfast Telegraph* itself. If there had been an Eleven Plus in goodies and baddies, I would have passed it, for a cert.

There were, you see, goodies and baddies everywhere. The world was divided up that way. It said so in the Bible and *Thunderbirds* and on the news. There were goodies and baddies in our street, in different parts of Belfast, in different countries throughout the world and right across the whole universe, in fact. So, it was important to be able to establish precisely who was good and who was bad. Generally speaking, goodies were friendly and baddies wanted to hurt you — so it was much safer if you stuck with goodies and avoided danger by staying away from baddies. They might even want to kill you, and hence it was sometimes better to try to kill them first, before they got a chance. As a pacifist paperboy, I struggled with the concept of a pre-emptive strike, although I had once used this approach most effectively, when my wee brother was threatening to scoff a whole jar of crunchy peanut butter, by striking him in the eye with my scout woggle.

Of course the most important starting point when learning about this moral spectrum was to recognise that you were always the goodie. You were a goodie because God had made you that way. It was great to be the goodie, except when your big brother called you a 'wee goody-goody' for six months after you had got saved at the caravan. It meant you were always in the right and much better than the baddies.

Obviously, Protestants were goodies and Catholics were baddies. Soldiers and policemen were goodies, while paramilitaries were baddies. Well, the UVF and the UDA were mainly baddies, but Mrs Piper always said that we would be 'lost without them to protect us, even though they're bad boys and rotten to the core'.

Wee hoods from down the road were always baddies, and grammar-school teachers were goodies — apart from the ones that nipped you under the arm for no reason and then taught you what a sadist was. Doctors and ministers and poke men were goodies, but bookies and priests and tick men were baddies. It goes without saying of course that paperboys were goodies, even Titch McCracken.

Sometimes though, it was very confusing. People who lived in caravans all year round were baddies, but people who lived in caravans for the Twelfth Fortnight were goodies. Men with long hair and beards who played drums in heavy-metal bands were baddies, because they worshipped the Devil – but men with short hair and moustaches who played drums in the flute band on the Twelfth were goodies, because they worshipped Ulster.

Wee African babies were goodies because they were starving to death, but we were goodies because we sent them money from our jumble sales. English people were mainly goodies, especially if they played for Man United, but if they wanted the troops out or were homos, then they were baddies. Scottish people were goodies because of tartan and the Bay City Rollers; Swedish people were goodies because of Agnetha. And my granny could not be moved in her view that all Germans were baddies, even though we had beaten them long ago and were still beating them in *It's a Knockout*.

Americans were special goodies, but it was complicated in the USA. They were mostly goodies, because of Walt Disney and the Osmonds (although my big brother said Donny was an even bigger goody-goody than me). I wondered if Donny had got saved on a bin at the caravan too, but then again, he was a Mormon – and Mrs Piper said they were baddies.

Americans were mainly goodies, because they made the best movies and had thousands of nuclear bombs pointing at the Russians, who were serious baddies. Americans were also goodies because they had dropped atomic bombs on Japan to win the war for us. American cowboys were goodies but American Indians were baddies, except for Tonto, because he helped the Lone Ranger. There were both goodies and baddies in *Starsky and Hutch*, but the two detectives were goodies of course, and always won. And I could not imagine anything in creation more goodie than Farrah Fawcett-Majors from *Charlie's Angels*, who I put up on my bedroom wall in a swimsuit. However, sometimes my father would shout at Americans on the news because they were sending money to the IRA to kill us, so I realised that some Americans must be baddies too. Which was okay, because I knew it was a very big country and they couldn't all be goodies.

Will Robinson in *Lost in Space* was an American and he was definitely a goodie, but Dr Zachary Smith on the same spaceship was a baddie and he was an American too. Of course maybe it didn't matter what country you came from when you were lost in outer space, and just because someone had an American accent didn't mean they actually came from America – like the DJs on Downtown Radio, for instance.

However, there was no doubt whatsoever about who the biggest baddies were. Everyone knew the facts. Russians, Provos and Daleks were the worst. They were the ones who wanted us dead the most. They were all powerful, showed no mercy and wanted to exterminate us. Of course, the Provos didn't have as many nuclear bombs and ray guns as the Russians and the Daleks, but they lived just over the Peace Wall so they were much more immediately threatening baddies.

I could understand why the IRA wanted the Brits out and all, but I couldn't understand how they decided who they were going to kill to get their way. It was dead scary, so it was. Loyalists were easy to understand because they just wanted to kill Catholics full stop, but the IRA had an ever-growing list of what they called 'legitimate targets'. Some of these I could understand – such as soldiers and policemen and taxi drivers – but when the list started to grow, to include cleaners and painters and decorators, I began to get worried. If the IRA wanted to kill you, they would get you, so you lived in hope that they wouldn't make you one of their legitimate targets. But the way things were going, it seemed, soon all Protestants, including paperboys, would be legitimate targets.

I started to get concerned when I noticed a pattern from the pages of my newspapers: the IRA were favouring attacks on milkmen and blowing up the Milk Marketing Board. I concluded that the milk industry must have been a major barrier to a United Ireland. It reminded me of Trevor's da's campaign to boycott Catholic cheese, so as to save Ulster. I wondered if the Provos thought all the cows were Protestants. I suppose that would have been hard to swallow, right enough. Or maybe they thought the Brits were putting secret drugs in the milk to turn us English, and that we would all wake up one day talking like on *Monty Python*: I guessed for a Provo that would be worse than being chopped up and turned into Frankenstein's monster in black and white on BBC 2 on a Friday night. I thought that if Trevor's da and a Provo ever got together in prison, they would probably have a lot in common –

as long as the Provo liked Elvis and absolutely no dairy products were present.

When the milkmen came under attack, I was more worried than I had ever been that the IRA were about to turn their sights on me. Milk was a delivery service, after all – and perilously close to my own profession. One night I had a nightmare that Ruairí Ó Brádaigh went on the news and said that paperboys delivering the *Belfast Telegraph* were now officially a part of the evil British propaganda war-machine thingy he was always talking about. I woke up in a terrible sweat. I had to look up at Farrah Fawcett-Majors for quite a while for some comfort before I could get back to sleep again.

But one night the bullets and bombs came closer to me than I had ever experienced until then. Ironically, it wasn't because I was a paperboy delivering propaganda for the British war-machine thingy. It was because I was a boy scout.

I liked being a scout. I had won Best Cub Scout in our troop in 1971. Normally Scouts was on a Wednesday night at eight o'clock, in the same Nissen Hut as the Westy Disco (except on Scouts night, the lights were on and there was no snogging). However, this week we were meeting early – at six o'clock – because we were going on a visit to the Belfast Fire Brigade Headquarters.

I was very excited about the prospect of seeing the fire engines up close, because the nearest I had ever been to one was watching *Trumpton*. I wanted to meet the brave firemen who dampened the flames of the bonfires, the buses and the Co-op Superstore. My excitement was subdued, however, by the problems the early start would cause me as a hard-working paperboy.

Determined to get everything fitted in, I rushed home from school, completed a particularly nasty algebra homework and learned my Latin verbs. Equipped with this absolutely crucial knowledge, I collected the papers from Oul' Mac, with even fewer words than usual. Then I dashed over hedges at speed and delivered all forty-eight *Belfast Telegraphs* faster than my wee brother on his space hopper at Sports Day. It was now half past five. I gulped down two fish fingers and a lump of Smash and swiftly changed into my scout uniform. This was a green jumper with yellow scarf held together with a woggle. Different scout troops had different colours of scarf, and it was unfortunate that our scarf was yellow, because when I saw the IRA marching on the news they had green shirts and yellow scarves too. They looked just like our Scouts in fact, except that they had dark glasses and guns, while we had woggles and first-aid badges.

By ten minutes to six, I was ready to leave: I would just have enough time to run down the hill to the West Circular Road, to join the other scouts. But as I opened the front door to leave, I heard a burst of gunfire and then another. It was much closer than usual. I felt my father put his hand on my shoulder to draw me back into the house. 'Houl your horses!' he said. 'Wait til we see where that was.'

Daddy got out the FM wireless and tuned into the army radio channel. You weren't really allowed to do this, but everyone did because you could always find out where the trouble was, even before the Downtown Radio news. We soon heard English voices using the code name 'Charlie'. Everybody knew that that meant our area. A voice said: 'Shooting on the West Circular Road!' That's where the scouts were. 'Shooting at the shops on the West Circular Road!' another voice crackled. This was just across the road from the Nissen hut.

'What if one of the scouts was over there buying chewing gum to bring on the trip?' I thought. That's what I had intended to do, if I hadn't been so late.

After a few more minutes of listening in to the secret conversations of the security forces, my father agreed that it was safe enough for me to go down the road to see what had happened with the Scouts. This was far more exciting than a visit to the fire station! As I ran down the hill, I could feel my heart beating twice as fast as usual. At first I thought this was down to the combination of sprinting and the excitement of the gun attack – but then it occurred to me that it might be my 'bad' heart, so I slowed down.

Suddenly, as I reached the bottom of the hill, the whole earth shook. The windows of the houses around me fell out onto the street. I froze on the pavement, clutching my woggle, and the whole world stopped, it seemed, apart from the sound of raining splintered glass. Then there was silence. Then alarms and sirens and men shouting and women screaming, and a foul, heavy black smoke everywhere. 'Danger, Will Robinson! Danger, Will Robinson!'

As I ventured around the corner onto the main road, I noticed some of my scout patrol crouching down on the ground behind a police cordon. There were still some windows falling out, and I saw that there were no tiles on the roof of the Post Office. I spotted wee Sammy Reeves in the crouching crowd. Sammy didn't wash much and never had a girlfriend, but he was exceptionally good at knots. His face looked very white beneath the grime.

'What happened?' I whispered to him. I don't know why I whispered, but no one was talking out loud.

'The Provos fired at the scouts waiting outside the hut, and we all had to duck down on the ground behind a car, and we nearly shit ourselves, and then the police came and shouted at us to get away fast cos they had planted a bomb at the shops, and as soon as we got back here, the whole f**kin' thing blew up!' wee Sammy panted.

I was raging. I had missed it! I had just missed it all by five minutes! Crestfallen and shaken, I walked home to hear what exactly had happened on the Downtown Radio news. I listened to the same bulletin every hour until midnight, even though the news didn't change. It just said there had been a gun attack on a group of scouts in West Belfast.

The next evening, it was on the front page of my papers, though no one in Belfast Royal Academy had even mentioned it in school that day. However, Titch McCracken was angrier than I had ever seen him, and he wasn't even in the scouts after he got thrown out for smoking in a tent at Crawfordsburn Country Park. Titch said it just proved that all Catholics hated us and supported the IRA, but later when I was in school with wee Thomas O'Hara and he was joking that I fancied Patricia Thompson, I was very certain he wouldn't want to hurt anybody.

For months, the rest of the scouts could talk about

how they had stood up to the IRA and escaped the bloody attack, but all I could say was that I had been doing my papers at the time. One of the older boys was awarded the Queen's Award for Scouts, for his courage in getting all the younger boys to hit the ground when the bullets started flying. Reverend Lowe said we should thank God that we were delivered from harm that night and that we should not be longing for more such incidents in our lives. He must have been reading our minds and somehow understood the strange fascination violence held for us.

For the rest of my career as a paperboy, when I sometimes heard gunfire in the distance while delivering my papers in the dark, I thought about the night they shot at the scouts. I worried that there might be other wee lads my age out there who weren't getting a chance to duck down in time. Wee lads just like me, not really understanding all the trouble going on all around them. Maybe they liked *Doctor Who* too. Maybe they had a lovely girlfriend like Sharon Burgess. Maybe they were hoping to go to the Bay City Rollers concert in the Ulster Hall. I could not forget the night the bullets missed the scouts and I had missed the bullets. I kept on wishing it would all end. But I knew it never would, so I did.

# CHAPTER TWELVE

## *a final verbal warning*

I got complacent, so I did. Now that my paperbag was black with experience, I began to cut corners and take risks. I was heading for a fall, as surely as the day I had slipped on Petra's poop, fallen against Mrs Grant's rose bush and torn my new tartan turn-ups out of John Frazer's. The same day I had run home crying and been spotted of course by Big Jaunty, who had told all the other paperboys the next day, when they had all laughed until they cried.

I had developed the sort of paperboy swagger that comes with the confidence of having delivered ten thousand papers with a completely clean disciplinary record. Among swaggers, the paperboy swagger was unique. It was more uncommon than a hard-man swagger, more routine than a marching-season swagger and less intimidating than a tartan-gang swagger. It was a swagger very much in its own right, and involved walking purposefully, while at the same time confidently swinging a heavy bag over one shoulder without losing your balance (no matter how high your platform shoes) whenever it swung back into place. Your shoulders would then continue an arrogant vertical and horizontal swaying motion, while one hand would remain fixed on the paperbag, holding it close to one leg. With your other hand, you would remove each newspaper from the paperbag, slapping and folding it aggressively against the other leg. It was paperboy poetry in motion. This complex ballet of the streets would be performed at great speed — unless you were in a bad mood because you had got the strap for your cheek and you weren't going to the caravan that weekend.

I had mastered the essentials of the job long ago, as well as identifying and honouring the importance of all of the more subtle dos and don'ts that were part of a paperboy's unwritten induction manual. These included the following immutable rules:

- Never throw newspapers towards a house like an American paperboy. This is Belfast: you could be mistaken for a petrol-bomber. Also, the paper might well get soaked or stolen.

- Do not rub your nose while doing the papers, as the black ink on your hands will create a Groucho Marx moustache on your face at the exact moment that a wee girl you fancy or your big brother is walking down the street. They will laugh and you will be humiliated.

- Do not over-fold your papers, or they will be too fat to fit through the standard letterbox.

- Do not attempt to deliver papers on a bike. The weight of your paperbag will inevitably shift your centre of gravity, so that you lose balance and crash into a prickly hedge, a brick wall, a rusty car, or all three.

- Do not fight with spring-loaded letterboxes. Accept that they will slice your fingers, no matter how good your delivery technique.

- Never attempt to deliver to houses with snarling dogs, especially if the owner says, 'Och, don't worry, love, he wouldn't touch ye.'

- Do not be seen jumping over fences between semi-detached houses. This will upset the more upwardly mobile customer by reminding them that, although they have risen from terrace to semi, they still live on the Shankill and as such have not yet achieved suburban detached status.

- Do keep ringing the doorbell if a curtain twitches and no one comes to the door, especially if they haven't paid their paper money for two weeks in a row.

- Do remember who is on holiday, so they do not return from Millisle to a newspaper mountain inside their front door.

- Do be nice to old ladies, including pretending you like their cats that scratch you, and be friendly with families who have a Ford Cortina and wash it every week, as these are the ones who are most likely to give you a good tip.

As my mastery of my trade became increasingly evident, I noticed how Oul' Mac began to look at me with a certain amount of awe. Clearly he had never before seen such flawlessness in a paperboy. I was never late; never once had I given him cheek; I had never stolen even a single penny. My employer's attitude to me changed from indifference to incredulity and then, finally, to admiration. I actually overheard him whispering the words, 'best f**kin' paperboy ever' to Mrs Mac once, as I walked into the shop with a bulging bag of tepid takings, fresh from my boots. And indeed, to Mrs Mac, I was approaching sainthood.

My customer complaint rate was exceptionally low. My clean slate had in fact been marred on a few occasions only, by unjust crumpled back-page complaints, and even then Oul' Mac had taken responsibility for the damaged goods as being van-related as opposed to bag-related. Each time, he had apologised to the customer, said it 'hadn't been the wee lad's fault', and given them a free *Ulster*. Even when customers sometimes complained unfairly – when, for example, it had actually been the postman who had spat on their step – I never told any of them where they could stick their *Belfast Telegraph* (at least not out loud), not even Mr Black from No. 13. And so the conflict had never escalated to management level and therefore Oul' Mac never even got to hear about it.

Of course, Mr Black had never liked me, since my very first paper round, when he had suggested I was too young for my vocation. The feeling was mutual: I didn't like the oul' get either. He was well known for being grumpy. My mother always described him as 'yet another ignorant wee Belfast man'. I took this to mean that there was a large pool of such men in our city. Mr Black's wife had died before I was born, and he had grown-up children in Canada and bad breath. He loved his greyhounds only.

One day, while happily engaged in my work and delivering his paper perfectly and on time, with one of the greyhounds tugging at the turn-up of my parallels, the same Mr Black told me off for whistling 'Fernando' by

ABBA. He said I should 'not be whistling no Republican song at his front door'. There was a line in 'Fernando' that went something like, 'How proud you were to fight for freedom in this land', and so Protestants thought Fernando was a Provo. I was certain, however, that Fernando, the song's hero, was fighting near the Rio Grande, because that rhymed with 'land' in the next line. ABBA spoke Swedish, so they liked easy English rhymes like that. I wasn't sure exactly where the Rio Grande was, but I was certain it wasn't anywhere near West Belfast. I supposed it might have been in the Bogside, but even then I was sure Fernando wasn't a Provo.

Mr Black's attack about my song choice seemed particularly unjust, since I wasn't even singing the questionable words of the song on the day in question: I was only whistling the tune. Anyway, I was in no doubt that the blonde one in ABBA, in whom I was developing an increasingly strong interest at the time, was much too nice to be on the other side's side. And I had never seen a woman look less like Bernadette Devlin. I couldn't work out whether Agnetha was a Protestant name or a Catholic name, but maybe Swedish was a different religion altogether, so it would be okay to marry her – although she was already married to Björn, which was a shame of course, because that was for ever.

As my professional complacence grew, I began to leave the occasional gate open behind me. If I suspected a customer was out at church or voting again, or if I otherwise judged they would not see my misdemeanour, I would wilfully leave their gate wide open. It felt good, dismissively letting it swing in the wind. I was a rebel now: no gate would dominate me. Of course, if there were small dogs or children that might escape onto the road and get knocked down by a bus, I was still very careful. But in less dangerous circumstances, I would sometimes belligerently let customers' gates swing on their squeaky hinges.

In the absence of witnesses, I would be only one of a range of suspects for the crime of a gate left swinging, and I knew that with my reputation, I would be at the back of the criminal queue. It could have been the bread boy, or the rag-and-bone man who shouted 'any oul regs?', or a scout 'bob-a-jobbing'. Or a politician canvassing or a Baptist giving out gospel tracts or a collector for the Loyalist prisoners. Any one of these would have made a better suspect than me. Yes, Christians, boy scouts and Loyalists were all more potentially aberrant than I was. If it came to a line-up in Tennent Street RUC station, I was sure I wouldn't be the one to be singled out: my reputation was secure, after all, and I knew that both Oul' and Mrs Mac would defend my innocence to the hilt. Once the pair of them had established the extent of my integrity, they had become invested in maintaining their belief in it.

I had become very smug. My family, the ones who knew me best, could recognise it only too well. 'Don't be so Mr Know-It-All now, love,' warned my mother. 'Stop being such a cocky wee shite!' ordered my father. 'Catch yerself on, dickhead!' chided my big brother. 'Wise up, wee lad,' said my wee brother.

But these challenges occurred behind closed doors, and

I was far from wising up. To my employers and customer base alike, I remained blameless. In my own mind I was beyond reproach. But pride, as the Reverend Lowe would have said, always comes before a fall ...

It happened on a Wednesday. The papers were lightest on a Monday and Wednesday, so these were generally my most complacent days. Lost in my smugness, I barely gave my professional responsibilities a thought that day. Although it was a school day, I was excited. On Wednesdays I had a violin lesson, and I played guitar at the Bible Union at lunchtime, so it would be a very musical day – although carrying both instruments to and from school on the bus was something of a balancing act. And even though I also had PE on Wednesdays and knew the tracksuited teacher would choose one of his rugger favourites to select the five-a-side teams and I would be one of the last to be picked, I didn't care, for today was to be the start of my acting career. I had auditioned for the school play, and the casting was to be announced during the after-school drama club that day. For, as well as being a violinist like Yehudi Menuhin and a guitarist like Paul McCartney, I had aspirations of becoming a great actor, like Roger Moore. The school play this year was to be *Tom Sawyer*, and I had auditioned for the parts of both Tom and Huckleberry Finn. I would have been happy with either part: I had already in fact begun to learn the lines of both. The drama club started at three o'clock and finished at four o'clock, so I reckoned that once I had landed my starring role and modestly accepted the congratulations of my supporting actors, I would have plenty of time to catch the bus home in time to do my paper round and then go to Scouts as usual.

'First of all, I have to say that you all did very well in your auditions,' began Miss Baron, our drama teacher, in a patronising manner. Miss Baron was young and blonde, and by far the most attractive teacher in the whole school. She was like Olivia Newton-John with chalk, and so she always got my complete attention. I was always determined to please Miss Baron.

'Aaahh, she's really nice … I like her … Is that blouse see-through, like the one Olivia Newton-John wears in my *Look-in* poster?' I found myself thinking. 'She's just letting the bad ones down gently, I suppose … That's really nice of her. If she just stood beside the window, I would know if it was see-through or not …'

'Not everyone can play a leading role, but there is always next year, of course,' Miss Baron continued authoritatively, interrupting the flow of my meandering thoughts.

I looked around me sympathetically at all the kids who were about to be disappointed. Miss Baron was right: they would always have next year. Miss Baron was always right.

'The part of Tom Sawyer will be played by … Thomas O'Hara,' were her next words. This was perfect casting: Thomas could use his real name, and he was already a good mate of mine, so we wouldn't have to act too hard at being Tom Sawyer and Huckleberry Finn. I patted my pal on the back magnanimously, as he grinned widely. My part was next.

'And the part of Huckleberry Finn will be played by … Patricia Thompson!' Silence. Then applause and congratulations for – Patricia bloody Thompson?!

*Excuse me?*
*Have I misheard?*
*I didn't get it.*
*I am not Huck?*
*I didn't get a part?*
*F\*\*k, I'm not Huck!*
*She has given my part to a … girl?*

I hate Patricia Thompson. I bet her da plays golf with the teachers and she lives up the Antrim Road. I bet no one from up the Shankill with a Ford Escort respray has ever been given a main part in a play in this snobby oul' school.

I hate that Miss Baron. She gets on like she thinks she's Olivia Newton-John, but she's an oul' boot, and she gave a boy's part to a girl. And Patricia Thompson already has breasts and … where is she going to put them?

I'm tellin'! Patricia Thompson is going to have to dress up as a boy. Miss Baron is trying to make Patricia Thompson into a homo – except a girl homo, if there is such a thing – and I'm going to tell my RE teacher because it sounds like a sin!

Somewhere amid the mists of my selfish anger and moral outrage, I hazily heard Miss Baron interrupt my internal ravings: 'The part of Boy Three, one of the boys who paints the fence for Tom, goes to Tony Macaulay.'

I was to be nothing more than a Boy Three – a bit part at Tom Sawyer's fence! Thomas O'Hara was to be the star, and I was nothing. This was humiliating. It was like Thomas got to be the new Doctor Who, if Tom Baker ever regenerated, while I got to be a Silurian stuck inside a rubber suit who then got zapped by the Sonic Screwdriver in the very first episode.

As far as I was concerned, Drama Club was over. But once we had been informed of the casting decisions, we had to do a read-through of the play. Thomas O'Hara had thirty lines to read for every one of mine. Patricia Thompson tried at first to put on a deep boy's voice for Huck, but Thomas O'Hara's voice hadn't broken yet, and it didn't sound right that the girl playing a boy had a deeper voice than the boy playing a boy. So Miss Baron told Patricia to just speak in her normal voice, so that Huck and Tom would sound the same. I rolled my eyes at this latest example of artistic misdirection, and I could not hide my disgust at Patricia's attempt at an American accent. The more she tried to sound authentically American, the more she sounded like a farmer from Ballymena. She had clearly never watched a single episode of *Sesame Street,* where you learned how to say the alphabet in American.

By four o'clock that afternoon, I just wanted to get out of there and get home to do my papers. At least my talents were appreciated at work, even if they were overlooked at school. As I left the school, it was already getting dark. It was raining, as usual, so I had to put up my blue duffle-coat hood. It wasn't properly waterproof, but it was so thick the rain didn't come through. I walked to my bus stop with my schoolbag over my shoulder, holding in one hand my guitar in its faux-leather case and, in the other, my violin case. It was just me and my instruments at this bus stop, where you could catch a bus into the city centre and, from the City Hall, take another bus up the Shankill. Most of the other thespians had gone to the Antrim Road bus stop. Patricia Thompson, for example, just had a short direct bus route home to her detached house — when her daddy didn't collect her in his Rover, that is. It wasn't fair.

After more than half an hour standing in the rain, during which time I was distracted by angry thoughts about Miss Baron and what would happen if Patricia Thompson broke her leg or if her minister were to receive an anonymous letter and didn't allow her to dress up as a boy, I realised that my bus was late. Sometimes the bus was late because of the Troubles, but it usually came within an hour, once the bomb-disposal men had had the chance to blow up the suspect device in the hijacked milk van in which it had been planted.

Another half hour passed, during which my mind wandered from time travel to meteorites to Agnetha. Then I realised that the bus was very late indeed. In fact, I knew that by now I would not make it home in time to collect my papers from Oul' Mac at the van. At this stage, I wasn't too concerned, however. I could still be home within an hour and deliver my *Tellys* a little late. I could blame the Provos; everyone would call them bastards, and everything would be okay. I searched in my pockets among the chewing gum and marbles for the two-pence piece I retained for such emergencies, and then I picked up my violin and guitar and calmly walked around the corner to the red public telephone box, in order to call home and ask my big brother to collect the papers.

It was only once I had managed to squeeze inside the phone box with both instruments and my schoolbag that I discovered it had been vandalised, and I had to

awkwardly extricate both myself and my luggage in a
reverse movement with my duffle-coat hood still up,
restricting my rear view. I daren't leave my guitar or
violin outside or, I was sure, they would be nicked for
Smithfield Market or a bonfire. I walked down the road
to the next telephone box, and it had been vandalised too.
Then on to the next, and the next: they were all broken.
Every telephone receiver had been torn from the wall and
the words 'Brits Out' scrawled everywhere. I knew these
were British Telecom telephones, but I had never realised
that a telephone box could be an instrument of British
oppression. Maybe they were bugged, like in James Bond?
Maybe if I did get through, 007 would be listening to my
every word, in case I was a Russian spy hiding plutonium
in my violin case?

As I considered several possible James Bond plot lines,
eventually, about a mile later down the road and halfway
to the City Hall, I found an intact telephone box. By this
stage, I was very wet and exhausted from walking and
manoeuvring in and out of countless telephone boxes,
weighed down with my schoolbooks and musical burdens.
I was starting to panic. If only I had had my own blue
police telephone box – my very own TARDIS – I would
be able to travel through time and space like the Doctor
and be home before I even left for school that morning.
Unless, of course, I pressed the wrong button and landed
on the planet Skaro and had to battle the Daleks who
were trying to take over the universe.

I was starting to think I might have to ask my big
brother to do my papers that night. I knew that he would

charge me double-time, which would mean less money to buy 'Love Is' cards for Sharon Burgess. I put my freezing fingers into the cold stainless-steel holes of the telephone dial and rang our home number. My mother answered quickly, and I immediately dropped my two pence into the money slot, hoping it would work properly this time, because often it didn't.

'Are you all right, love?' Mammy asked excitedly. 'The buses are all off! The UDA are burning them all to stop a United Ireland, and Paisley says we're going down the Dublin Road! And you and your brother aren't home from your drama and his rugby, and it's terrible! And the roads are all blocked with barricades, and your daddy can't even get the car down the road to collect youse, and youse'll have to walk home the night in the dark. And I'm worried sick, and they'll pick on you with your violin, and your father's up til a hundred ...'

'Mammy, I'm going to be late for my papers,' I interrupted, realising that my two pence would only give me a few precious minutes before the pips went and I was cut off. 'Can you go round and get my papers from the van, and I'll do them when I get home or, if I'm not home in time, ask ...'

Beep-beep-beep-beep. I could hear the pips and then the line went dead. The conversation was over. I hoped my mother had got the important message. I wasn't too worried about walking home in the dark, and I knew I wouldn't be going anywhere near the Dublin Road, but I didn't like the suggestion that I would be picked on for carrying my violin, and I just hoped Mammy would collect my papers and my big brother would deliver them when he got home.

I walked for streets and streets into the city centre and then for miles and miles up the Shankill, towards home in the dark in the rain in a duffle coat with a guitar case in one hand, a violin case in the other hand and a schoolbag over my shoulder. I must have stood out, but no one picked on me. In fact, no one paid me any attention at all. There were much more interesting sights to behold: burning buses, barricades blocking the roads, tartan gangs with petrol bombs, police and soldiers in riot gear with guns pointing in every direction. The public-transport network was being torched to save Ulster. My concerns were insignificant in relation to these cataclysmic events, but my feet were sore.

As I reached the top of the Shankill Road, there was a further delay. Due to several riots on the main road and adjoining streets, not only were vehicles being prevented from going any further, but so were pedestrians. The RUC had blocked off all the roads and the pavements, and so I could go no further. There was only one way up the Shankill to my home and that was up the Shankill! There was no alternative route: I was stuck. It was nine o'clock, and I had long since given up any ambition of delivering my own papers that evening, but at least my big brother would have carried out substitution duties fairly adequately. Unless of course my mother had done them – but she had sounded much too distressed to be thinking about my papers.

I stood quietly among a gathering crowd of similarly stranded pedestrians waiting for the all-clear. I was wet and tired, but mainly bored. Some of the others were talking excitedly about the drama that had unfolded throughout the day. They seemed to be enjoying it all, in fact. I was just bored, however. Then several Elvis fans with tattoos began to move among us, whispering important information in privileged ears. While the gathering crowd speculated about a rumoured IRA invasion and how Paisley would save us, I just stood and dreamed of being Scott Tracy on *Thunderbird 2* – although not with puppet strings.

Suddenly, I was struck across the back of the head and my duffle-coat hood fell down. I turned around to see if I had been picked on by a violin-hating Loyalist, but I got a huge shock, because standing there behind me in the stranded crowd was my big brother with his schoolbag and rugby kit. With muck from a scrum still on his face, he exclaimed, 'Look at the state of you, with a guitar and violin and a duffle coat! What are ye like, ya big fruit?!'

I was glad to see him too. But then it dawned on me: if he was here and hadn't made it home yet either, then no one would have done my papers! Unless of course my parents had done them, and that was unlikely. I began to realise that I was in big trouble. The perfect paperboy had fallen! I imagined the raised voices of forty-eight angry customers against one errant paperboy. I pictured one extremely angry Oul' Mac and one deeply disappointed Mrs Mac. I was doomed. This was the stuff of instant dismissal. It was gross misconduct. My career was at an end. When I explained the situation to my big brother, he wasn't reassuring.

'Oul' Mac'll kill ye!' he said, as the RUC finally let us through the site of the now-quelled street unrest.

The two of us arrived home just after ten o'clock, to be greeted by jubilant and relieved parents. My mother opened the front door tearfully and hugged us very tightly. During this embrace, all I could do was look over Mammy's shoulder at the pile of forty-eight fresh *Belfast Telegraphs* with the white cord uncut around them. They were just sitting there sullenly, undelivered. I felt sick. I dropped an instrument from each hand, knowing that tomorrow I would have to face the music.

I slept remarkably well that night, however. The exhaustion of my mammoth trek home outweighed the anxiety provoked by the prospect of facing Oul' Mac and the sound of shooting outside. The next day at school, I developed a clever plan. If I wasn't sacked instantly, I would deliver Wednesday's paper and Thursday's paper both together! If anyone asked, I would blame the rioters from down the Road, and Oul' Mac would never hear about it, and I would survive.

Sure enough, when Oul' Mac arrived with the Thursday night Sixth Editions, there was no mention of my misdemeanour. I knew as soon as I saw him that he wasn't angry. His cigarette ash formed a long drooping protuberance from his mouth – this was not the cigarette of an agitated man. I was relieved: obviously no one had complained. My customers must have assumed that Oul' Mac had not been able to get the papers through the barricades the previous night. This had happened before, when the roads had been barricaded to keep us British, and for most people it was worth the sacrifice.

I gathered the Thursday *Tellys* into my paperbag as usual, but then I ran around the corner to our house, where I added the Wednesday night editions into the bag. I thought my shoulder would break under the strain, but this was a minor discomfort, compared to the potential trauma of being dismissed at such an early stage in my career. And so I began to deliver two newspapers to every house. I tried to fold them into one to take the bad look off them, but together, they were too thick to fit through the letterboxes.

As I proceeded on my paper round, a series of doors began to open behind me. A third of the way up the street, half the doors were open. It was like when a band marched up the street – except not such a happy occasion.

'That's last night's, son,' said one bemused customer.

'What are you playing at?' said another.

'Where were ye last night, love?' enquired another.

It wasn't going well. My plan had backfired. By trying to deliver Wednesday with Thursday, I had revealed to the street that there having been no paper on Wednesday was my fault and was not down to the rioters. Mr Black, of course, dealt the final blow.

'That's yesterday's paper,' he said viciously. 'Did no one ever tell you in your grammar-school education that a daily newspaper is worthless the day after it is published?'

'Sorry, I was late home last night after school drama club and the riots,' I foolishly attempted to explain.

'Don't give me that, wee lad,' Mr Black replied, scornfully. 'You can take yesterday's paper back now. I don't want it and you can tell Oul' Mac I'll not be paying for it, so you can stick it up your arse.'

This man would have tested the restraint of the most resolute pacifist paperboy.

At that moment, a short queue developed in front of me, all of them dissatisfied customers returning Wednesday night *Tellys*, reminding me that they would not be paying for these. I was receiving as many newspapers back as I had delivered. My paperbag was now as heavy as ever. This was a disaster: the issue of who would be paying for the undelivered papers immediately brought Oul' Mac back into the equation, and I knew it was only a matter of time before someone phoned the newsagent's shop to complain. I never found out who it was, but I assumed it was oul' Mr Black who had betrayed me.

The next evening, Oul' Mac arrived in the van as usual. As he stopped, he put the handbrake on more aggressively than usual, it seemed. I could feel the screech in my teeth. This meant trouble. Oul' Mac scanned the waiting crowd of paperboys, until his eyes fixed upon me. He stubbed out his cigarette in the ashtray on the dashboard and jumped out of the van with the vigour of a man of half his age. This was a very bad sign. He headed straight for me.

I had planned to accept my dismissal with dignity. I wouldn't cry, and I wouldn't tell my employer where he could stick his paper round. I was clinging on to the hope that he might at least provide me with a satisfactory reference for my next employer. If not, I was destined for signing on in Snugville Street forever.

'You, here! Nigh!' Oul' Mac pointed at me and shouted. He sounded like Davros, the creator of the Daleks.

'What sort of a wee blurt tries to deliver the Wednesday night *Telly* on a Thursday night?' he enquired. I hung my head in shame. It was a reasonable question, except for the 'wee blurt' bit.

'I'm sorry Mr Mac, I was at drama, and the buses were off ...' I attempted to explain, before he unexpectedly interrupted.

'You were at what? Drama?' my employer asked in rhetorical disbelief. 'I'll have f**kin' Laurence Olivier doing the papers next!'

Then, to my surprise, he laughed and shook his head. I feared one of his looser teeth would fall out, but they hung in there as precariously as my contract of employment.

Oul' Mac then looked at me in the eye very seriously and said in low voice: 'Last chance, wee lad. Happens again and you're out on yer arse! And you're paying for them!'

I was relieved. It wasn't to be instant dismissal after all. This was my final verbal warning. It knocked the complacency out of me and reduced my swagger considerably. I delivered my papers with eyes facing down for the next few weeks, until both customers and line manager forgot all. I paid for all forty-eight newspapers out of my weekly wages, and I donated the batch of Wednesday night editions to the church wastepaper scheme to raise money for the Biafran babies. It was a sort of penance. I had learned the hard way, so I had.

# CHAPTER THIRTEEN

## *sharing streets with soldiers*

Very few people tramped the streets of the Upper Shankill as much as a paperboy. Compared to me, even Orangemen were half-hearted and seasonal part-timers. My fellow professionals, those who also marched the streets on a daily basis, were postmen, milkmen, bread men and soldiers. The postman delivered bills from the Great Universal Club Book, letters from your pen pal in New Zealand, sea-monkey eggs and your Eleven Plus results. The milkman woke you up very early – even before *Farming Roundup* on Downtown Radio – with the comforting hum of his electric milk float. These early-morning sounds once triggered a dream that I was Wilfred Owen from English class, writing a poem about 'the clink of giggling glass bottles as yet blissfully unaware of their impending metamorphosis into petrol bombs'. The bread men delivered delicious barmbrack loaf for butter smothering, as well as soda and potato bread for the mammoth Ulster fry your father cooked on a Saturday morning. The soldiers were different, though. They weren't delivering anything, and they were usually the only ones with guns.

The soldiers had been a constant presence on our street for as long as I could remember. Apart from Thomas O'Hara from BRA and Patrick Walsh from the School of Music, they were the only people I had ever met who weren't the same as me. Nearly everyone else was white and Protestant and British. When I was younger, I used to think everyone in the whole world was white and Protestant and British – even Doctor Who, and he was from the planet Gallifrey.

The soldiers brought the outside world to our well-scrubbed doorsteps. They usually had English accents like people on TV, except not as posh. Sometimes the soldiers on our street had Scottish accents, and sometimes they were black. I soon learned that there were different regiments that came and went, but the only ones I could ever distinguish were the Scotchies, because they talked like the Bay City Rollers, and the Paras, because Catholics hated them the most because of Bloody Sunday, and so we had to like them the best.

If you asked the soldiers to show you their guns, they would say things like, 'All right, mate!' just like Norman Wisdom in a black-and-white movie. I was fascinated by all the stuff they carried. The gear they had was heavier than a paperbag on a Friday night. They had berets, bullet proof vests and radios, and they had the most impressive big boots that I was sure would be able to accommodate an absolute fortune of coins.

All the women in our street loved the soldiers. Especially Mrs Piper, who adored them. 'Och, God love the wee craters, they're awful young and they don't even know what they're doin' over here, and them dirty IRA brutes is trying till kill them!' she would say.

Mrs Piper talked about the soldiers as if they were children, which I thought was strange, because children weren't allowed guns.

The soldiers were here to protect us from the IRA, so during the day when the men were out at work, all the women in our street would invite them in for a cup of tea. I noticed that they never asked the soldiers to come in when their own men were around, and I realised that this must have been something to do with male rivalry. Perhaps it would have been like Sharon Burgess inviting Donny Osmond into the Westy Disco for a packet of Tayto Cheese & Onion crisps and brown lemonade while I was there. I don't know in fact how the soldiers ever made it up our street in a single day, because everyone wanted to give them tea and buns. I for one was jealous. No one ever offered a paperboy a cup of tea. Not even Mrs Grant ever asked me into her scullery for so much as a piece and jam, although actually she never asked the soldiers in either, because her Richard was always off work and at home with his chest.

Aware of the preferential treatment given to soldiers compared to paperboys, I was sufficiently irked to ask my big brother one time, 'How would they stop the IRA invadin'' our street if they're always halfway through a gravy ring and balancin' a cup and saucer on their khaki knees?'

'Wise a bap, wee lad!' was my brother's thoughtful reply.

This tradition of making tea for the soldiers soon became something of a competition in our street, as the women vied for position, each hoping to establish their home as the premier tea house. My mother played her part in the contest admirably, with an apple tart that was particularly popular with the Paras, but she and the other women in the street soon realised that they could never compete with Auntie

Mabel's amazing baking skills, and so eventually they graciously allowed her to claim the crown. The secret of her success was the allure of her tray bakes. All the women knew how to make an excellent tray bake, but Auntie Mabel's were the toast of the Town Women's Guild. For all its might, the British Army was defenceless to battle against the seduction of her caramel squares. And so, every day, Auntie Mabel's small sitting room would be packed with English accents and scones and uniforms and rifles and buttered wheaten slices with homemade blackberry jam from up the fields. The Paras would put their rifles in the umbrella stand and get extra butterfly cakes.

The soldiers were usually very nice in our street. When they spoke to me, it made me think of when the British explorers with pith helmets talked to the natives in the jungle in Tarzan movies: they were very polite, but they didn't seem to understand our ways very well. Though, of course, you had to be careful when the soldiers were around. If you were out playing with a toy gun in the dark, they might shoot you. We weren't allowed toy guns for Christmas any more, which was no big sacrifice for me, as I was, after all, the only pacifist paperboy in West Belfast and I hated guns, apart from ray guns for killing aliens, of course.

I noticed from my cross-community conversations with Patrick Walsh, between a mauling of Mozart movements at the School of Music, that while Protestants called the British Army 'the soldiers', Catholics preferred to call them 'the Brits' and that while Protestants seemed to like the soldiers, Catholics would not give a Brit so much as a

crumb of a caramel square. Patrick told me stories of how
the Brits stopped you and searched you, beat you up and
raided your house, and then shot your cousin in the face
with a plastic bullet – but Mrs Piper always said they only
did that to Provo sympathisers that wanted to kill them.
While I thought Patrick was telling the truth, it still hurt
when he wrote 'Brits Out' in the boys' toilets, because I
thought that meant me too.

One of my most prized possessions was a bit of bomb,
so it was. This was a heavy and jagged piece of shrapnel
from a German bomb that my father had found as a boy
up the Glencairn on the slopes of Divis Mountain after
an air raid during the Blitz on Belfast in the 1940s. You
could still see the shape of the crater in the field where
the stray bomb had landed thirty years earlier. Dad had
kept the shrapnel safe ever since and had even painted it
with some silvery anti-corrosion paint he had borrowed
from the foundry. I knew I could have picked up a piece of
shrapnel around Belfast any day at that time, but this relic
from the Second World War fascinated me. I imagined a
German bomber called Fritz flying over Belfast in a fighter
plane and sneezing, accidentally pressing the bomb button
before reaching the shipyard. And the bomb falling down
on Glencairn before the new estate was built and the
paramilitaries took over, and it exploding in a farmer's
field and scaring the cows and all.

I had taken the shrapnel into BRA for a history project
on the Second World War, and, once the history teacher
had been reassured that it was a vintage rather than a more
contemporary bomb fragment, he was very impressed

indeed. And so the shrapnel sat until the end of term on the artefact table at the back of the classroom, alongside ration books and gas masks.

My bit of bomb had always achieved a positive reaction, and so when my father casually suggested I should show it to the soldiers some day, 'because they would like that sort of thing', I resolved to share my shrapnel with them the very next time they were in our street. The following day, just as I was finishing the papers, I spotted an army patrol at the bottom of the street getting out of a tank and being barked at by Petra. 'Brilliant! I'm gonna show the soldiers my bomb,' I said to myself, delightedly.

I ran to the house, hurled my empty, pitch-black paperbag under the stairs (where it would hang on a hook beside the hoover and the strap), and quickly shot upstairs to my bedroom to retrieve my striking museum piece. By the time I had bounded down the stairs again and was back out into the street, the army patrol had already successfully executed a pincer movement up the street towards Auntie Mabel's house, with two soldiers already marching past her nasturtium borders en route to her front door. I followed behind, eagerly clutching my shrapnel so close to my Bay City Rollers T-shirt that the silver paint rubbed off on Woody's nose.

'Och, come on in, love,' called Auntie Mabel, who was always as warm as her freshest scones. 'I'll make you a juice and a wee biccie,' she added, predictably. 'Do ye wanna talk to the soldiers, love?' she then asked.

I nodded, and, as she headed for the scullery to boil the kettle and pile up the tray bakes and sugar lumps, I was left alone in the sitting room with many china ornaments, four lace doilies, two soldiers and two guns.

'All right, mate?' said one soldier, who looked like he hadn't started shaving yet.

'All right mate?' echoed the other one, who had a scar on his trigger finger.

'I've got a bomb to show ye!' the quiet Belfast boy with ink-dirtied fingers announced.

The two looked a little startled and moved back very quickly when I suddenly thrust the metal object towards them. The one who had never shaved jumped back so sharply in fact that he dropped his rifle on Auntie Mabel's hearth and knocked over her china dog. Thankfully the dog wasn't broken and the gun didn't go off.

'Jesus Christ, what the hell is that?' asked the one with the scar. I assumed from the profanity that he wasn't a wee good livin' soldier.

'It's a bit of German bomb that Hitler dropped on Belfast during the war, so he did, and my daddy found it up the fields and kept it and said I should show it to yousens because he says yousens would like that sort of thing, so youse would,' I replied.

The soldier with the scar took the shrapnel and inspected it briefly. He then handed it back to me, saying, 'Pull the other one, mate!' and his colleague joined him in a mocking laugh.

I was affronted. It had never occurred to me that anyone would doubt the authenticity of my artefact, least of all two professionals in the field of war.

'But it is from a real bomb, my Daddy found it and says

it is from a German bomber from the Blitz and sure, feel how heavy it is …'

I attempted to explain, as I once again offered the fragment for further investigation to the fresh-faced one.

He refused to take it and turned to his mate and said, sniggering, 'This is what they're all like, mate. You can't trust them. They're always trying to pull the wool over your eyes.'

I was confused and upset. The only wool in the room was in Auntie Mabel's knitting basket behind the pouffe, and I wasn't trying to pull it anywhere near their eyes. Although I could see a knitting needle sticking out of the basket, and I had a sudden urge to utilise it as weapon against my mockers, except they had guns and I was the only pacifist paperboy in West Belfast, and … Why were they talking about me as 'they' and as if I wasn't even there?!

Then the one with the scar on his trigger finger said, 'Do you fink we is f**kin' fick, mate?'

I dared not answer truthfully. Now I was angry. I had never before heard the 'f' word in Auntie Mabel's sitting room – this was disrespectful. This was outrageous, like saying 'shite' in church.

The tirade of arrogant ignorance continued: 'What would the Germans have been doin' bombin' Belfast, anyway? They wasn't even interested in bleedin' Ireland!'

I tried to explain that the Germans had bombed Belfast because our shipyard built lots of ships for the war and that we were part of Britain, but my protectors just laughed. I was clearly wasting my time trying to educate them. Maybe they didn't do history in English schools, or maybe these two hadn't got their Eleven Plus.

'Leave it out, mate, you is talking fairy stories, and we ain't bitin'!' said the stubbleless one. All of this sounded so much more insulting when delivered with the added authority of an English accent. It was like being told you were officially wrong by Angela Rippon herself on BBC News.

I stormed out of Auntie Mabel's sitting room cradling my rejected shimmering artefact. It had lost some of its lustre, and not just because some of the silver paint had rubbed off on Woody's nose.

As I ran out the front door, I could hear Auntie Mabel calling after me, 'What about your juice and Jammie Dodgers, love?'

I was disappointed, humiliated and very angry. I knew the soldiers were here to stop the IRA from killing me, and that I should be grateful, but I couldn't help wishing those two would choke on one of Auntie Mabel's caramel squares. Maybe Patrick Walsh was right.

'Brits!' I thought, crossly.

A few weeks later, my relationship with the British Army would deteriorate still further. I was staying late after school for drama practice. It was the dress rehearsal for *The Adventures of Tom Sawyer and Huckleberry Finn*. For weeks, I had stayed late every Wednesday, risking not being on time for my papers, to dutifully fulfil my limited obligations as supporting actor to Thomas O'Hara, who, I had to admit, had turned out to be a very good Tom Sawyer. Patricia Thompson was still a girl with breasts playing Huck, which should of course have been my part. Now that we were at the dress-rehearsal stage, it was more obvious than ever that Huckleberry Finn had breasts. However, the more I looked at Patricia's chest to check out that this was indeed a visible travesty, the less angry I felt towards her, somehow. It was strange.

This bizarre change – from hostility to Patricia Thompson's part, to attraction to her parts – was noted onstage during the dress rehearsal by wee Thomas, and during the fence-painting scene, he whispered in my ear, 'Will you stop staring at Huck's diddies, ya pervert!'

I stopped looking immediately, as I was certain that if Tom Sawyer had noticed that I was staring at Huckleberry Finn's breasts, someone in the audience would be sure to accuse me of some sort of sin.

As I left the said dress rehearsal, it was wet and dark as usual. My thoughts were wandering from having homework and doing my papers to how great it would be to have my own TARDIS to travel home through time and space, maybe with Patricia Thompson as my companion. And so I was unaware that a British soldier had been closely observing my departure from the school. The side gate of the school premises was always closed at this time of the day, and so I had jumped over the wall for a shortcut. This was no problem for a paperboy well experienced in the art of wall-jumping, but as I landed on the pavement, the soldier apprehended me immediately.

'What you doin'?' he asked, aggressively.

'I've just been at the final dress rehearsal for *The Adventures of Tom Sawyer and Huckleberry Finn* in my school in there,' I replied honestly.

'Uhhh?' my interlocutor grunted, a puzzled look on his face.

It was then I realised how this must look. I wasn't wearing my school uniform, and I had just jumped over the wall. 'This poor soldier thinks I'm a terrorist,' I thought, 'although I am wearing a blue duffle coat and grammar-school scarf.'

I looked more like Paddington Bear than a Provo.

'Name?' the soldier demanded.

'My name's Tony Macaulay,' I answered honestly.

'Where do you live?' he asked next.

'At the top of the Shankill,' I replied honestly. No sooner had I said it than I realised this was not the wisest answer.

'Up against the wall!' my interrogator ordered. I began to wonder if this was what Patrick Walsh called 'harassment by the British war machine'. I obliged, however, and turned around, putting my hands against the wall as the soldier began to search me from duffle-coat hood to toe. He was quite rough, going through my pockets and shouting at me to keep my legs apart and 'not to f\*\*kin' move'. When he had finished, I was permitted to turn around again, to watch him go through the various suspicious objects he had found on my person.

First he inspected my latest packet of melted white sweetie mice. I prayed he wouldn't think it was Semtex. Next, he examined my *Captain Scarlet* badge. *Captain Scarlet* was an indestructible puppet, like in *Thunderbirds*, except he worked for Spectrum and fought the Mysterons. On his cap, he would wear a badge with the Spectrum symbol, and I had got a similar badge free in my Sugar Puffs.

'What's this?' asked the soldier suspiciously.

I was surprised. Maybe they didn't get *Captain Scarlet* in England.

'It's a Spectrum badge from *Captain Scarlet* who fights the Mysterons from Mars,' I answered honestly.

'Uhhh?' he grunted again, with that puzzled look on his face.

The soldier reminded me of the wee hood my father had decked with the pickaxe handle: even though he was in control of me, he looked scared. I could not take my eyes off his rifle. He was holding it near the trigger. 'Danger, Will Robinson! Danger, Will Robinson!'

'Don't lie – it's paramilitary!' he hissed. The badge was red, white and blue. He threw it on the pavement and stamped on it angrily with his substantial boots. Now I was really getting worried. According to Patrick Walsh, the Brits would stop you, harass you, put you up against a wall, then search you, beat you up and shoot you in the face with a plastic bullet. I was already halfway through the process, and the getting-beaten-up part was coming next.

'I'm not a paramilitary, I'm a paperboy,' I said politely but nervously.

'Uhhh?' he grunted again. I seemed to bemuse the soldier. He was looking at me the way Mr Spock would look at strange new life forms in *Star Trek*.

'I was just acting a boy painting the fence in school with Tom and Huck, and I need to get home soon for the papers or Oul' Mac'll sack me!' I explained.

Before he had the chance to utter yet another 'Uhhh?', his superior officer arrived on the scene.

'It's okay, soldjah,' the officer said in a posh voice, 'that's an Orange school – no problems here. Let the little chap go!' He looked and talked liked the sort of army officer they made fun of in *Monty Python*. I had to suppress a smile as I imagined him breaking out into a silly walk.

I had never thought of BRA as an 'Orange' school before. Nearly everyone there was Protestant, but they tended to look down on Orangemen: most people at BRA were more interested in rugger and golf than marching and band parades. Nevertheless, although this description of my school by the posh soldier was an inaccurate one, I appreciated the fact that his upper-class intervention would save me from getting a beating for my affiliation with Spectrum. At least, I hoped so anyway. I wondered what the officer would have said about Patrick Walsh's school and what would have happened to Patrick in similar circumstances.

'Run along now, young chap!' he said.

'And don't f**kin' do it again!' my young oppressor shouted after me. I had no idea what he didn't want me to do again, because I didn't know what I had done wrong in the first place, apart from having a *Captain Scarlet* badge in my pocket from my Sugar Puffs.

I was becoming aware of the injustices of life. First, a wee hood had stolen my *Thunderbirds* badge, and now the British Army had destroyed my *Captain Scarlet* insignia. Could a boy not live a life free from badge mistreatment?

As I ran for the bus, so as to ensure I got home in time to do my papers, I was angry with the soldiers again. I knew they were on our side and they were here to stop the IRA from killing me, but now I was really starting to dislike them. As a pacifist paperboy, I had always been against men in balaclavas and dark glasses with guns but the army were the official ones with guns, and I was starting to mistrust them too.

'Maybe men should be the same as children,' I thought, 'and none of them should be allowed to have guns. Apart from ray guns, of course.'

# CHAPTER FOURTEEN

## *save the children*

I was shocked, so I was. I was really shocked. No one had ever told me.

I was standing in the telephone box with my paperbag half full, in a vain attempt to shelter from the merciless hailstones that were suddenly raining from the sky. They had already penetrated my Harrington jacket and made the tartan run, so that the red dye had come off on my Bay City Rollers T-shirt and all over Les McKeown's face. This gave the impression that Les was wearing lipstick, like the lead singer from Sweet. Though at least the ash from Titch McCracken's cremated newspapers was by now almost completely eradicated from the stone floor beneath me. I opened the pages of that night's *Belly Telly* to pass the time until the worst of the hail was over and I could resume my professional responsibilities.

The hailstones were, however, still spitting at me ferociously through a few broken windowpanes that had suffered the consequences of Philip Ferris's catapult practice, as I began to read a report in the newspaper about starving babies in Biafra. All at once, I came across words I had never seen or heard before: they said that there was enough food in the world to feed everyone! I was shocked. If there was enough food to go around everyone in the whole world, then why were the Biafran babies still starving? I couldn't quite grasp it. It wasn't fair!

The report said there was enough food to feed us all, but that the rich countries didn't share it properly with the poor countries. I couldn't believe it — why not? I was certain that if anyone in Belfast heard that wee babies were starving to death anywhere in our city, we would share our Smash and fish fingers with them right away, even if they 'kicked with the wrong foot'. At BRA, if someone forgot their dinner money or their lunchbox, everyone would help out with a few crisps and a Dairylea triangle. In our street, if my mother ran out of sugar, she was always able to borrow some from Auntie Emma, and if any of the other paperboys was ever a *Telly* short, one of us would always donate him a spare one.

Maybe it was because Africa was too far away to share with. Maybe planes didn't go to Africa. But I was sure I remembered Princess Anne going to Africa on a plane to go on safari with *Blue Peter*. I really couldn't understand what the problem could possibly be. America was even further away than Africa in my geography atlas, and people got on planes all the time to go over there and give their money to Disneyland. So why could we not bring enough money or even enough food on a plane to stop the Biafran babies from starving to death? It wasn't fair, I thought, and it didn't make sense. Something had to be done. This injustice required action!

As soon as the hailstones stopped, I emerged determinedly from the telephone box, like Superman with a paperbag, resolving that I, for one, would share my riches with Africa. I knew I was just a wee lad from up the Shankill, but I wanted to follow in the footsteps of Cliff Richard and

Mother Teresa (even though he was old-fashioned and she was a Catholic): I was going to help the poorest people in the world!

So, where did I first go to look for an opportunity to save humanity? The back pages of *Look-in*, of course. By this stage, I had already answered most of the ads that appeared there every week, including one for the ABBA Fan Club and one for a silver pen with a personalised rubber stamp with your name on, hidden in a secret compartment inside. (When I read in the ABBA fan-club newsletter how much Björn said he adored Agnetha, I vengefully stamped my name all over his face.)

It was only a few weeks after I had resolved to help the babies in Africa that I saw a fresh notice squeezed in between the ads selling sea monkeys that died and those relating to my former hero, Charles Atlas. This was an advertisement from the Save the Children Fund, asking me to join their 'Roundabout Club', to raise money for the poor wee children. I responded earnestly and immediately by sending a 50p postal order. A few weeks later, I received my very own fund-raising pack.

My Roundabout Club folder included a letter signed by a real Sir in England, who was the boss of saving the children. No one in our house had ever received a letter from a Sir before, so I had to show it to everyone. My wee brother wanted to know if the Sir was related to Sir Lancelot in the King Arthur cartoons. And my granny was most impressed. 'I always thought you were the swankiest wee grandson, love,' she said tearfully.

My father was the least enthusiastic. 'No son of mine

will ever be tugging his forelock to no English Sir!' he proclaimed. I hadn't a clue what he was talking about.

The Roundabout Club pack also included a badge, stickers and a membership book, where you earned points for all the money you raised to save the children. The more money you sent to save children, the more points you would get: you could win a bronze, a silver and a gold badge – like in the Olympics. I quickly got the hang of it, and every few months, I sent a 50p postal order from my surplus tips. It wasn't long before I earned a bronze badge.

However, every time I received a Roundabout Club newsletter, I noticed there were lots of photos of very clean children in England, getting their picture taken with the Sir and being presented with their gold badges, because they had raised fifty pounds doing sponsored pony rides. I could never have dreamed of raising that much money, because we didn't have ponies in Belfast – although you could have a ride on a wooden horse on Mickey Marley's roundabout in Corn Market on a Saturday afternoon for only 10p. I decided, however, that I could come up with an exciting plan for a major fundraising event, which might at least earn me a silver badge. It might even result in me getting my picture taken with the real Sir, and could possibly save lots more children in the process.

As I delivered my papers each night in the shadows, I mulled over various ideas – even though I knew that too much thinking while delivering the papers could be hazardous. There was always the danger of standing in Petra's poop, or not spotting a wee hood lurking in an entry.

I was already an experienced fund-raiser, in fact. During the annual Bob-a-Job Week for the Scouts, I would wash cars and pull out weeds from nasturtium borders for a whole six days (not on the Sunday though, because that would have been a sin). I also raised a pound every year by collecting one hundred pennies from all my aunties and putting a hundred pinpricks in a Presbyterian Orphan Society card. As I contemplated all my fundraising options, I considered a sponsored *Opportunity Knocks,* like on TV, with me as a young Hughie Green – but then I knew nobody would enter, except Irene Maxwell singing David Cassidy out of tune. I also came up with the idea of a sponsored football 'keepy-uppy' competition, but then I knew my big brother would only win and everyone would say it was fixed. I even thought about ringing Gloria Hunniford at UTV to ask her to do a bingo session in the church hall, but I knew I wouldn't be allowed: bingo was bad because it was gambling.

Eventually, after a careful evaluation of all the possibilities, I settled on a marvellous plan for my first fund-raising project for the babies in Africa. It would be the best fund-raiser our street had ever seen: a jumble sale. Not just any ordinary jumble sale, however, but a wonderful innovation which would feature musical speakers and hot dogs. Not only would I be selling high-quality second-hand merchandise, I would also be offering musical treats and tasty refreshments! This was taking the concept of the humble jumble sale to a whole new level. I would give all those wee girls and their ponies in England a good run for their money!

My harmonious sale, complete with culinary delights, would take a lot of serious planning and preparation. First of all, I had to climb up into the darkness of the roof space, in order to select appropriate stock from boxes of old stuff. I loved it up there in the attic. It felt safe and was packed with faded boxes full of old black-and-white photographs of my father with hair, and my mother and her wee sister, Auntie Doris, looking all young and glamorous like film stars in old movies on Saturday afternoons on TV. As I rummaged through my family's relics from the 1950s and 1960s, I felt as if I had travelled back in time in the TARDIS. I discovered ancient 78s by Jim Reeves, and dusty hardback books about birds and fish and flowers. I found old granny china ornaments of hedgehogs and fox terriers wrapped up in ancient *Belfast Telegraph* pages, delivered no doubt by some long-grown-up paperboy. To my delight, I uncovered real treasure in the form of an old *Doctor Who* annual from years ago, when the Doctor was an old man with white hair and he didn't even have a scarf. From all of this, I retrieved the most saleable items and priced them sensibly.

Next I would set my wares out on the kitchen table at our front gate to attract passing customers, all the while imagining that I was a window dresser for the Christmas display in Anderson and McAuley on Royal Avenue. To add to the whole attraction, my masterstroke would be to borrow the speakers from the Westy Disco, plug them into our stereogram and blast out the Hit Parade through the sitting-room windows and into the street. The Upper Shankill had never seen a jumble sale like this before. You would be able to buy a slightly chipped ornament, an Elvis

78 and an old book about flowers, while singing along to 'Mamma Mia'. If you didn't like ABBA, you would be able to pay 5p to request a different song. It would be a bit like a jukebox, except I would have to run into the sitting room to change the record on the stereogram. The biggest innovation of all, however, would be the ingenious addition of hot dogs to the traditional jumble-sale format. No one in our street had ever attempted this before. I calculated that if I bought a dozen sausages and an Ormo pan loaf and borrowed the tomato ketchup from my Auntie Hettie, and sold twelve hot dogs at 20p each, then I could more than double my money and get my silver badge – I mean, save lots of children.

On the day itself, however, it was the hot dogs that turned out to be the biggest practical challenge. I found myself having to grill the sausages in the kitchen while at the same time serving customers at the kitchen table at the gate, in between running in and out of the sitting room to change the records on the stereogram. This proved to be much more demanding than delivering forty-eight *Belfast Telegraphs* in the rain.

I had realised prior to the big day that I would require additional manpower for my enterprise, and accordingly had initiated a staff-recruitment process within my family. It seemed that my parents would not be available. My father would be doing overtime at the foundry for a new hall-and-stairs carpet, and my mother had a silk kimono dress to finish on the sewing machine for a swanky woman up the Malone Road for some big dinner dance she was going to at the Chimney Corner hotel. My big brother declined my offer of gainful employment with the words, 'Wise a bap, wee lad!', though he kindly donated a pair of old red clackers for the jumble sale. (Clackers were basically two snooker balls on two strings that you banged together and up and down very fast until they made a loud, clacking noise and bruised your wrists. They had been the latest thing but they had gone out of fashion very quickly, like hula-hoops and the Peace People.)

Thankfully, my wee brother had been an enthusiastic recruit to my team. I quickly delegated to him some of the duties of running in and out of the house, which he happily did at great speed on his bright-orange space hopper. Of course, he was too young to go near the sausages grilling in the oven in the kitchen, but he was good at fetching knives. He knew how to change records on the stereogram, although, as it turned out, he did put on 'Two Little Boys' by Rolf Harris far too many times.

I had to cook the sausages myself. I decided to grill instead of fry, because in my experience the grill was less likely to go on fire than the frying pan. I knew you were supposed to fry most foods, but I decided to make an exception for the hot-dog sausages on this occasion, because I would need to be able to cook them while at the same time selling goods and taking musical requests. I had purchased two packets of Cookstown sausages because Geordie Best ate them on commercials on UTV. Geordie Best was the only real superstar from Belfast, and the only one with a Northern Ireland accent on TV who didn't talk about fighting. He was the best footballer on earth, and he liked parties and Miss Worlds. I wasn't very good at football, and my big brother said I 'couldn't kick back doors', but Geordie was still a hero to me. So I figured that if my hot dogs had Geordie Best sausages in them, they would sell like hot cakes.

On the day of the great jumble sale, my first customer was oul' Mr Butler who was bad with his nerves. He bought an ancient Elvis 78 called 'Heartbreak Hotel'. It didn't sound to me like it would cheer him up much, but he seemed very satisfied anyway. Mr Butler then ordered a hot dog with red sauce. When I put the sausage into this first hot dog, it had looked a little too pink, but even though it wasn't fully cooked, I served it up anyway – because I wanted all of my potential customers to hear that I served fast food like McDonald's in America. I smothered the sausage with extra ketchup, so that Mr Butler wouldn't notice the pink meat. He seemed to thoroughly enjoy it.

My next customer was Titch McCracken. When he arrived at the kitchen table sitting out in the street, Titch's eyes immediately fixed on the red clackers.

'Much for the clackers?' he enquired brusquely.

'Fifty nupes,' I replied, with an air of assurance.

Titch opened his plastic wallet. It was the same wallet he always had with him on bus trips and at the tuck shop at the Westy Disco. There were never any pound notes in it, but it always contained a small picture of Olivia Newton-John and a wee square wrapper that said 'Durex' on it. I could understand why you would want to have Olivia in your wallet, but I couldn't fathom why you would keep the same wee square wrapper in your wallet for years and never even take it out. Of course, on this occasion too, the wallet was bereft of cash. Ever since being sacked by Oul'

Mac over the incendiary incident in the phone box, wee Titch had struggled to make ends meet, and he had been barred from the local Mace shop for stealing sweetie mice. 'Wise-ick!' was his response to my perfectly reasonable price for the pair of clackers.

But before this business negotiation could get into full swing, I heard my wee brother shouting out from the kitchen. 'Quick! Quick! The sausages is all on fire!' he cried alarmingly.

I rushed indoors to the kitchen, and, sure enough, the sausage fat in the grill had ignited. There was smoke everywhere: it looked like the stage on *Top of the Pops*. I feared my jumble sale would turn into a smoke-damage sale, like in the Co-op Superstore! I had learned in chemistry class and on *Blue Peter* not to throw water over a fire in the kitchen, so I bravely lifted the whole grill pan by its hot handle and threw it out the back door into the garden. Sausages rained down on the clover-ridden lawn. For a moment I wondered if this was what it felt like to throw a petrol bomb (except a bomb wouldn't have the sausages of course). The grill pan landed hard, crushing my father's favourite rose bush, so I knew I was in trouble — but at least I hadn't set the house on fire. It was the lesser of two evils.

Acting quickly, I retrieved the least burnt sausages from the ground. I inserted the most heavily carbonised pork through the wire into Snowball's hutch. Interestingly, although Snowball was a particularly obese albino rabbit, he remained steadfastly vegetarian, even when exposed to such high levels of temptation. I then washed the surviving sausages in the sink to clean the soil and grass off and left them on the draining board to dry.

Once the emergency was over, I returned to my neglected customers in the street. By the time I returned to my sales station at the table, however, both Titch McCracken and the red clackers had mysteriously vanished. Later, he steadfastly denied that he had stolen these objects of desire, but the sudden appearance of bruises on his wrist the next day gave him away. As natural justice would have it, a few weeks later, Titch ended up in the Royal with a broken wrist. I was sure it had been the clackers.

By this stage, the marvellous jumble sale was deteriorating into chaos. I had sold very little, lost merchandise to my shoplifting mate and burned my Geordie Best sausages. However, just as I was about to admit defeat and close up shop, a crowd of girls came walking down the street. Linking arms happily, they were chewing gum and singing:

> We are the millie girls,
> We wear our hair in curls,
> We wear our skinners to our knees.
> We neither smoke nor drink,
> (That's what our parents think,)
> We are the Shankill millie girls …

I immediately recognised the gift of a marketing opportunity. I dashed indoors, put Donny Osmond on the stereogram and turned the speakers up full blast. It worked! The girls were enthralled. They stopped at my table in the street, with eyes wide open. They had never heard Donny in the street before.

'Have you any Rollers, wee lad?' they enquired in unison.

'All their albums,' I replied triumphantly.

'Class!' said the leader of the gang, as she twirled a long stretch of chewing gum around her forefinger.

Within seconds, I had made 50 pence from Bay City Rollers requests alone. The girls weren't really too interested in the jumble sale, but they enjoyed the music, and I was sure they would go for the hot dogs.

'I'm goin' to see the Rollers at the Ulster Hall, so I am,' I said, knowing this would enhance the prospect of further sales.

'Class!' said the leader of the gang, as she scraped the chewing gum from her forefinger into her mouth with her two front teeth. 'And are you going to be on the Westy Disco float in the Lord Mayor's Show?' she asked.

'Yeah, my Ma and Da are organising it,' I replied proudly.

By this stage of the conversation with the millie group, I was feeling quite the lad – until, that is, the next question hit me right between the eyes.

'Are you seein' Sharon Burgess?' asked one of the smaller girls I had never even met before.

'Aye!' I replied, blushing.

'She's only going out with you because she fancies your big brother, ya know,' my interlocutor announced with great authority.

In that instant, everything stopped. This was front-page headline news. For a second my whole world stopped turning. The record-player turntable on the stereogram in the sitting room was still going obstinately around, however. I could only vaguely hear the words of 'Bye Bye, Baby' in the background. I pretended to ignore the wee millie girl's comment. I said nothing in reply — but I would relive and remember those words for hours and days afterwards. This was worse than having a bad heart — it was having a broken heart.

However, for the present, I had to put my acting skills into practice. Miss Baron would have been very proud of me: I simply pretended nothing had happened, and I offered the gang of girls a hot dog with a Geordie Best sausage. They were delighted, and I took an order for four hot dogs. Fortunately this corresponded exactly with the number of surviving sausages now drying out on the draining board in the kitchen. I had now learned my lesson on leaving store security compromised, so this time I sent my wee brother inside with instructions to carry out the sausages and bread on our faux-brass patterned tray. He eagerly obeyed, and within ten seconds, he re-emerged from the house, bounding up the pathway, clinging on to one ear of his bright-orange space hopper with one hand and carrying the tray of Geordie Best sausages and an Ormo pan loaf with the other.

Unfortunately my wee brother's enthusiasm had resulted in an unnecessary level of acceleration, and, as he sped closer and closer to the jumble-sale table, I realised that another disaster was about to unfold. With the sound of a drum solo from Woody playing in the background, my wee brother crashed into my table, chipping the formica and launching the entire contents of the jumble sale into

the road, like an *Apollo* lift-off. To make matters worse, he
lost balance completely on impact with the table, and the
tray carrying the hot dogs continued on its trajectory into
the middle of the road.

Our street was strewn with smashed glass, books, broken
records, bread and sausages. It looked like North Street
after a bomb in Woolworths. My wee brother had landed
right on top of me, knocking me over, so that I ended up
horizontal on the pavement on top of half an Ormo pan
loaf and a bottle of tomato ketchup. The sauce splattered all
over the back of my Harrington jacket. I couldn't believe
it. I had only just got rid of the smell of boke from the
Larne–Stranraer Ferry from my most favourite article of
clothing, and now I would have to splash on even more
Brut all over to mask the smell of tomato sauce.

But sure, it didn't matter what I smelt like anymore, I
suddenly thought. Sharon Burgess was going to two-time
me with my big brother, and he would just love that, while
I would be chucked and humiliated. Meanwhile, the gang
of millie girls ran away up the street, giggling guiltily as if
they were afraid of being blamed for something. Then, I'm
afraid my pacifist principles were once again compromised:
I kicked my wee brother hard on the shins until he stopped
laughing and started crying.

I looked around at the devastation before me. It wasn't
fair. I looked across at the bright-orange space hopper now
lying still in the middle of the road. Its big, smiley face
seemed to be looking straight at me. Petra the dog was
standing beside it, wagging her tail, happily eating up all
the remaining Geordie Best sausages.

I had tried my best, but on my first amazing fundraising venture, I had just ended up losing money. I would never get my silver badge or get my picture taken with a real English Sir, and no children whatsoever would be saved. The space hopper smiled a huge, mocking smile at me. It wasn't fair. Life wasn't fair, so it wasn't. The world wasn't fair.

# CHAPTER FIFTEEN

## *peace in the papers*

One of the best things about growing up in the Upper Shankill was that you could go 'up the fields'. This was the end of Belfast, where urban sprawl met threatened countryside. However, for us, up the fields represented much more than just a glimpse of pastoral beauty. It was up the fields that my father had fled as a boy when Hitler bombed Belfast. Thousands camped out in those fields during the Blitz. Then I was told that up the fields would be our escape route too, should the IRA burn us out to get rid of the last Protestants from West Belfast. I imagined choosing which of my James Bond Corgi cars and *Doctor Who* annuals to carry with me the night the IRA would burn our house down. I pictured a wee Catholic boy called Seamus using my paperbag and delivering *The Irish News* and the *RTÉ Guide* the next day.

So 'up the fields' was a safe haven. But there was adventure and a sense of danger there too. One remaining farm perched above our estate. It was a declining rural remnant of another era. The farmer there resented the runny-nosed children with Belfast accents. No doubt we personified for him the cheek of the encroaching city. It was this farmer's fields that presented so much excitement to us, for there were risks attached to going up the fields. You could be chased by the angry farmer himself, or his incensed bull – which was rumoured to have killed a wee boy once.

If you went too far into the fields above the north or the west of the city, then you could be chased by vengeful Celtic supporters coming across the mountain from Ligoniel or New Barnsley. There were no peace walls up the mountain yet, so you never knew how safe you were. Every trip up the fields was an adventure.

In the lower fields, we collected bucketloads of blackberries every year. Our fingers would be stained with a fusion of blackberry juice and blood from thorn pricks. I became an expert blackberry picker. It was like delivering papers, only in reverse: instead of emptying a large canvas bag, you filled up a small plastic bag. After years of practice, I could spot the perfect blackberry, ripe for the picking. If the berry was bulging black, it would burst in your fingers and be lost in a juicy mess – my fingers would be stained black. If a berry was too green, it would be immovable, and its thorns would prick your fingers until they bled. My fingers would be stained red. The perfect ripe blackberry was halfway between the two. After a day of successful blackberry-picking and paper delivery, my fingers would be a healthy hue of dark purple. The mothers of the estate would fill jam jars with their homemade blackberry jam. Up the fields was also the place where we plundered frogspawn and newts from the few remaining mountain streams and introduced them to life in the same jam jars, once we had emptied them for a piece and jam.

Every July, we built the bonfire on the lower field. I would spend hours going round the doors for wood. My customers were most generous. If I had delivered the papers proficiently through the winter months, I would be rewarded with ample flammable material come July. The main donations were small broken crates and sticks and cut-down hydrangea bushes, but the most generous donors gave us whole back doors, broken guiders and old wardrobes. My main bonfire duties, apart from wood collection, were building the 'boney' and guarding it at night with the older boys.

Building a boney was an intricate task. We spent hours getting the base right, so that it would not collapse as the wood piled up. I have no doubt that we learned more about physics and engineering at the boney than in school. A passing dad would do the occasional safety inspection, and now and again a mum would bring us juice and Jammie Dodgers as we rested from our labours in the sunshine. Rival bonfire gangs in neighbouring streets were a constant threat: if they got through your defences and lit your boney before the Eleventh Night, you would have to endure a whole year of taunts and humiliation. And so guarding duties were very important, and we would build a wee guardhouse in the centre of the bonfire in which to sleep at night. I would get very upset every July because my parents never allowed me to sleep inside the bonfire. How unreasonable of them!

Some summer days I was so distracted by my duties at the boney that I almost forgot about my primary occupation – the papers – unless I heard the distant roar of Oul' Mac's van, or Mrs McDonnell, who got a *Beano* and a *Dandy* for her grandchildren, popped her head through the bushes and asked, 'Are there no papers the night, love?' Then I would dash to the van, heart beating fast, fearing an imminent disciplinary procedure from Oul' Mac.

I loved the Eleventh Night. You would sometimes get a tip from the Orangemen customers, the ones who always put their flags out. On that night, their faces would seem to light up like a bonfire too. The preparation and the atmosphere up the fields was in fact far more enjoyable than watching marching bands the next day, playing boring old-fashioned music that you never heard on *Top of the Pops*. I used to climb up the fields every Eleventh Night and watch the warm glow of bonfires all over Belfast, when weeks of hard work would go up in glorious smoke in the space of a few hours. I remember the smell of damp wood smoking and foil-covered potatoes baking. There was no underage drinking, and no burning of tyres or Irish tricolours at our 'boney'. Apparently, it was the 'dirt down the Road' who did that.

The upper fields of the Black Mountain were more remote and mysterious than those nearest to us. I remember my father returning once from a walk up there with a prehistoric flint arrowhead, like in my school history book. He said there was a 'something-o-lithic' quarry up there. I imagined a colony of surviving cavemen, hiding out in undiscovered caves above us. Some people also said that's where the UDA had their meetings.

The first day I climbed to the top of the Black Mountain, it was almost as exciting as *Thunderbird 3* taking off from Tracy Island. I was both exhilarated and exhausted. As I hiked up to the higher fields with my cousin Mark, I imagined I was climbing Mount Everest, like Sir Edmund Thingummy. After hours of tramping through 'cows'

clap' and mud, over hawthorn bush and painful bramble
and through unfamiliar heather and moss, we arrived at
the top.

I was the whole way up the fields for the first time ever! I
was thrilled: the views were breathtaking and spectacular. I
could see all of Belfast: the dome of the City Hall where old
men argued; the Co-op Superstore still smouldering in York
Street; the big Samson and Goliath cranes in the shipyard
where the good jobs were; the unknown enemy territory
of Ardoyne. I could see across Belfast Lough, to where the
rich people lived, before you got to the caravan in Millisle,
and in the distance I could even see where the Mountains of
Mourne swept down to the slot machines, candy floss and
'kiss-me-quick' hats. From this vantage point, you could see
across the peace lines to strange alien places you had never
been – like in *Star Trek*, except that, unlike Captain James T.
Kirk, you would never boldly go where no one from your
side had gone before.

However, the greatest sight of all from the top of the
mountain was the massive Divis television transmitter
that gave us the BBC and was on the news regularly
for being repaired or bombed. It was famous – a single
celebrity tower on the top of Belfast. Soldiers guarded
the transmitter, like it was their boney, so you couldn't
get too near, but it was still impressive to me to be close
to something so powerful. (The BBC was very posh and
authoritative, though none of the politicians seemed to
like it. Even the newsreaders from Northern Ireland
spoke with strange English accents: they pronounced
every 'ing', but didn't pronounce their 'r's. They would

say we were listening to 'Radio Ulstah', or watching 'BBC Nawthan Ahland').

* * *

There was one day in particular up the fields that I would never forget. It was a spring day, and I was up there with my big brother, collecting dandelion leaves for Snowball, the obese albino rabbit. On the way back down the lower fields, we met Roberta and Mandy, two wee girls from our estate, who were happily taking turns on the rope swing.

Roberta Ross and Mandy Brown were two older girls who lived in the next street and who both still got *Bunty*, even though they were of *Jackie* age. Their street was the one that led you up the fields: it was on a steep hill, so it was hard work to carry bonfire wood up there in the summer, but great fun to slide down on the lid of a biscuit tin in the winter. The rope swing the girls were playing on was slung from the tallest tree in the lowest field. It was far more exciting than the ageing, vandalised playground swings in Woodvale Park. (The park used to have a wonderfully sickening roundabout and a cold steel slide as well, but it all got wrecked in the Troubles.) Meanwhile, up the fields, this magnificent swing was like something from *The Adventures of Tom Sawyer*. Made of thick strong rope borrowed by a dad from the shipyard, it had a huge knot at the bottom to sit on. When you fell off the tree swing, you usually ended up in the Royal for stitches.

Roberta's father was a milkman who got up very early in the morning, and Mandy's mother took Keep Fit with plump pensioners in the church hall. Mandy fancied my big brother, so the two wee girls giggled as we approached them at the swing. My big brother provoked a lot of reactions in me, but giggling wasn't one of them. I just couldn't understand girls.

'Hiya!' said Mandy, swinging happily. Roberta giggled.

''Bout ye?' said my big brother. He spat out his Wrigley's in a very manly way.

'Mandy fancies you!' announced Roberta indiscreetly.

My big brother did not reply directly. Instead, he picked up a small stone and fired it at the bough of the tree, knocking off a small piece of bark. Mandy jumped a little, but looked impressed. Throwing stones was a sign of virility in West Belfast.

Roberta and Mandy weren't cheeky or millies, so I thought they would be easy to impress. I picked up a slightly larger stone and also threw it at the poor, embattled tree. My aim wasn't as good as my big brother's, so I missed the tree, and Mandy had to duck as my stone flew past her head into the field, missing its target by several miles. The two girls giggled again. This giggle had a different tone to the one they had given in response to my big brother, though. He was a genius at aiming footballs, rugby balls, cricket balls and stones. I was only good at aiming newspapers through letterboxes.

As if to consolidate my humiliation, my big brother then picked up a large, impressive piece of cement from the remains of last year's boney. There was still white ash on it, which covered his hands and his Wrangler jacket. Although he now looked like Auntie Mabel after she had been mixing

216

flour to make buns for the soldiers, the girls still looked at him respectfully. No mocking giggles for my big brother. He hurled the lump of cement with both hands, and the projectile ploughed into the bough of the tree and knocked off several small and hopeless green shoots. The rope swing shuddered, and Mandy seemed to shudder too at this display of masculinity. I knew instinctively that it was my turn. Not to be outdone, I looked around the debris of last year's bonfire. There were some rusty springs that were all that remained of the old mattress that Mrs Porter had given us when her husband died, but I realised that these would be too small to make an impact.

'What's that you've got in your pocket?' asked Mandy, who had suddenly noticed the dandelion leaves falling out of the pockets of my parallels.

'It's dandelion leaves for our Snowball, so it is,' I replied innocently. The giggling erupted once more.

'Dandelion leaves make you wet the bed, ya know, wee boy,' taunted Mandy. There then ensued a musical chorus of 'Wet the bed, wet the bed', and eventually my traitorous big brother joined in: 'Wet the bed, wet the bed, wet the bed ... '

It didn't make sense. How could a weed from up the fields impact on my bladder function while I was in my bed? Maybe I had missed that page in my biology book. Maybe that's what made Snowball pee on his straw so much. I hadn't wet the bed for years, although I had recently spilled some Lucozade on the sheets when I was in bed with the chickenpox. Anyway, now I understood why my big brother wasn't carrying any dandelion leaves in his pockets. He had plucked dozens of leaves, but they had all been stuffed into my pockets. I was clearly intended to be the beast of burden for all potentially embarrassing materials. I was the ass for kicking.

By this stage, I was becoming desperate to save face. I needed a big stone, and I needed one now. I suddenly spied a red brick from last year's bonfire debris. It had been used to hold down the sides of our tent the night before the Eleventh Night, when I had been allowed to sleep beside the boney (rather than inside it). I lifted the heavy half-brick and flung it at the tree. Once again, however, it missed its intended destination, and once again Mandy had to duck. As she fell off the swing into the ashy dust below, the red brick continued on its tragic trajectory and hit poor Roberta Ross on the head. 'Oh f**k!' said my big brother and disappeared into the distance in an instant, like a summarily sacked paperboy.

Mandy was now lying on the ground, holding her scratched leg and crying. Roberta looked up at me with a trickle of blood on her forehead, and, as she stared at me, the water came to her eyes too. I had red brick on my hands.

I froze on the spot. I had made two wee girls cry. I had made two wee girls bleed! I was in trouble. This was the worst thing I had ever done in my life – worse even than stealing sweetie mice from the youth-club tuck shop when the minister's wife's back was turned to open a new box of Tayto Cheese & Onion. I felt guilt and fear in equal measure. And I was ashamed.

'You're dead!' shouted Mandy.

I couldn't disagree.

'Her Da is gonna kill you!' she continued.

*Not if my Da kills me first*, I thought.

What had happened to me? I had turned from rabbit nurturer to terrorist in seconds!

Roberta just looked at me pitifully and cried, until the blood and tears blended on her cheeks. She didn't shout or scream or call me a 'cheeky wee bastard' or anything – and that just made it worse.

*What am I going to do?* I thought. I had to consider the right course of action. Roberta's da was a milkman, so he was probably a hard man because milkmen were legitimate targets. But it was the afternoon, so he was probably in bed right now … Having evaluated all of my options, I took a moral decision. I ran away.

I didn't set foot in that wee girl's street for two years after this, in case her da got me. I had to find an alternative route to the July bonfire through Mr Beattie's hedge, and I missed a whole winter season of street-sliding on my biscuit-tin lid. I had a recurring nightmare of Roberta's da coming to our front door with an angry face, shaking a milk bottle in my face and threatening to split my head like his wee girl's. But it never came to pass. Any hope, however, of a career progression from paperboy to milk boy was shattered.

Interestingly, my big brother displayed great loyalty, by not revealing any of the details of the assault to my parents, so I got off with it. I felt guilty though. I still feel guilty. But somehow I learned something that day up the fields. The bloodied face of Roberta Ross was unforgettable. I worked out that I didn't want to do anything like that ever again. Sure, there were enough people drawing blood in

Belfast, and too many of them seemed to enjoy it. So I chose a different path – the path of the pacifist paperboy. It all happened up the fields. The same fields where I watched peace from a distance, in 1976.

* * *

It was 28 August, and there had been no big stories or elections for a while, just the usual marches and murders. While the papers were usually a bit lighter in the summer, on this day there were shoulder-breaking extra pages. Oul' Mac had arrived late with the delivery because the crowds were still causing a traffic jam on the Shankill Road. Although he was shouting and saying 'f**k' even more than usual, there was no danger of Oul' Mac's van being hijacked today. For this was the day that the Catholic women of the Falls Road would walk across the Peace Line and when the Protestant women of the Shankill Road would join them to walk together for peace. This was unheard of.

I first stumbled upon the suggestion that this miracle might actually happen on a recent front page of one of my *Belly Tellys*. I was so shocked when I read this news that I stopped still on the pavement mid-delivery and my paperbag dropped off my shoulder, landing perilously close to a recent dirty deposit made by Petra, our street's now legendary labrador.

I wasn't used to miracles. Protestants and Catholics didn't mix deliberately, unless they were rioting at the Peace Line, or arguing on *Scene Around Six*; unless there were petrol bombs or politicians present. We weren't allowed to live in the same street; we weren't allowed to go to school together; we weren't allowed to get married; and we even got blown up in different pubs. And, after that, we would be buried in different graveyards. My granda's family were buried in an old cemetery that was divided between the two sides: when I went to visit my dead relatives, I noticed there were no Virgin Marys on our side of the cemetery. I wondered if the corpses were building peace walls underground, but I was pretty sure that wouldn't matter quite so much down there.

Of course, sometimes Catholics and Protestants couldn't avoid ending up in the same place together – like when all the kids from the Falls and the Shankill had to go to the Cupar Street Clinic to get a polio vaccination. In the waiting room, the mothers would talk away to each other like everything was all right, agree that it was terrible what was going on, so it was, and that it was a small minority on both sides that was causing all the trouble, so it was. They would not dare to get any more specific, for fear there would be an unhealthy exchange in a clinic with such large needles present. But although we queued together for polio injections on the Peace Line, that wasn't the same as marching together for peace in public. You were supposed to march against them, not with them!

On that sunny August day, the front page of the *Belfast Telegraph* had a picture showing our mountain, the Black Mountain, rising behind a 25,000 strong throng of widely flared women in Woodvale Park. In the same picture, I could make out the trees in the park where my name was carved alongside that of Sharon Burgess. Elton John and Kiki Dee were at No.1, but it seemed possible now that Sharon might go breaking my heart anyway. In the grainy image on the front page of my papers, I could also see the fields on the slopes of the Black Mountain in the background, where, only a few hours ago, I had sat and watched the huge rally for peace. I had been a tiny dot up there behind it all.

Most of the women in our street, including my mother, had decided to go to the rally. My mother said she would know some of the Catholic women from the Falls Road, because she used to sew with them before the Troubles. The few women in our street who stayed behind that day were the ones who believed that God or the man they voted for – or both – would disapprove of marching for peace with Catholics, or 'Roman Catholics', as Mrs Piper called them. She always corrected you for saying 'Catholic', which was almost as wicked as saying 'Derry' instead of Londonderry'. But for a brief interval that summer, the Mrs Pipers were the minority.

Of course, most of the men stayed at home. It seemed that peace was women's work. Manning vigilante barricades, hijacking buses and joining the UDA was for my gender. Titch McCracken said you were only a real Ulsterman if you were prepared to fight and die to keep Ulster British. I was prepared to defend the earth from an alien invasion, but that was as far as I was willing to go.

As I climbed up the fields that day, I wondered why a boy could only watch peace. Reaching the higher fields, I was amazed at the sight of the crowds in Woodvale Park that afternoon, and moved by the sound of singing and cheering.

A strange mix of laughter and the refrain of 'Abide with Me' was bouncing off the Black Mountain that day. This was unbelievable.

Unexpectedly, I found myself weeping. I was used to the echo of bomb blasts and gunfire. Were we really capable of this? It seemed a lot harder than fighting. This was the answer. The Troubles would be over soon. One day the killing would stop. There would be no more bombs at the shops and no more soldiers on the streets. And everyone would agree that all the fighting had been a waste of life. I was living in hope, so I was.

# CHAPTER SIXTEEN

## *puppy love*

I hated spots, so I did. An enormous zit always seemed to erupt on the end of my nose just in time for the Westy Disco on a Saturday night. Sharon Burgess would have been too sensitive to my feelings to have ever drawn attention to such things, but I feared my big red nose could be seen throbbing in the dark, like the disco lights that flashed in time with 'Shang-a-Lang'. So I applied Clearasil lotion to my pitted face every day, in spite of the typical taunts I knew this would draw from my big brother. I even tried to burn off my spots with Brut. I already of course had some personal experience of the proven fiery effects of aftershave on sensitive skin, and so I splashed it all over my spots. It hurt, but it didn't work. It just made the spots grow larger.

I wanted to look good for my first sweetheart: I needed to retain her affections under possible threat. The disturbing revelations of the wee millie at my jumble-sale fiasco were still ringing in my ears: 'She's only going out with you because she fancies your big brother, ya know.'

I repeated these words in my head many times thereafter. Even when I tried to forget them, they wouldn't go away. It was like putting ABBA's *Greatest Hits* on repeat on the stereogram in the sitting room and not being able to get 'I Do, I Do, I Do …' out of your head for the rest of the day.

I never mentioned any of this to Sharon Burgess, because I believed she was innocent until proven guilty. It would have been very out of character for the lovely Sharon Burgess to be going out with a wee lad just to get close to his big brother. She was too perfect to do anything like that. Her deep brown eyes were too bright and honest to be clouded by any such deceit. Her skin was soft and beautiful, and she never had any spots. Sharon Burgess was like a Miss World, but younger, in parallels and without a tiara. Our family watched *Miss World* on TV every year. It was real family viewing. My mother admired the evening gowns, and my father enjoyed the swimsuits. My brothers and I were also more than susceptible to the charms of this beauty contest, and we enjoyed picking our favourite ones every year, like in the *Eurovision Song Contest*. One year, however, we were sent to bed early for fighting, after my big brother accused me of staring at Miss Argentina's diddies.

To bring up the damaging gossip I had heard about my own personal Miss Upper Shankill and my big brother carried the risk of accusing my sweetheart of an unproven crime. People in Belfast got accused of things they hadn't done all the time, so I was determined not to make the same mistake myself. It would have been as bad as suggesting that Sarah Jane Smith only assisted the Doctor in the TARDIS because she fancied the Master. This was just as unthinkable, and to suggest such a thing would just have made Sharon chuck me. I did, however, closely observe any interactions she had with my big brother – but I couldn't detect any signs of adoration. I even secretly looked up the problem page of Irene Maxwell's *Jackie* one week before I delivered it, to see if there were any letters from a girl called Sharon in Belfast who fancied her boyfriend's big brother. I also consoled myself with the thought that my big brother wasn't interested in my girlfriend anyway, because she was too young for him and he preferred girls who did gymnastics.

To look handsome enough for Sharon Burgess necessitated well-pressed parallels, polished platforms and feathered hair from His n' Hers beside the graveyard where Sharon's own mother did the feathering. But I knew I could only ever be superficially handsome without perfect skin like David Cassidy and perfect teeth like Donny Osmond. So I began a war on acne. Although I spent many hours on the battlefield in front of the bathroom mirror, I never seemed to win a strategic victory. I tried squeezing the most persistent spots, but that just made them bigger and then I would get shouted at by my mother for splatting zit pus on the bathroom mirror. Pinching the most stubborn spot was like trying to push an already torn newspaper through a customer's letterbox: it just made things worse. I found myself facing defeat on a daily basis.

Then, as if the acne wasn't bad enough, I began to notice that my teeth were growing in a very strange manner. I noticed this change over the course of a few months, during my daily inspection of my face in the mirror, when I would be searching hopefully but in vain for signs of new hard hairs on my upper lip. I would also scan my skin for newly erupted or potentially threatening spot sites. At first, it was barely noticeable, with my upper canines growing down like those of a normal human, but after a while I observed that they kept growing further and further downwards. To my horror,

I realised that I was developing fangs! It was ghoulish – I was beginning to look like Dracula. At Halloween I didn't have to buy plastic fangs in a Lucky Bag any more, because my real teeth were becoming monstrous enough. I was turning into the only good livin' vampire in history. How could this be happening? My mother was next to notice this dental deformity, and I knew it was becoming obvious when my big brother began referring to me as 'Fang'. I knew a visit to the dreaded dentist was inevitable.

The dentist's surgery was in a big old three-storey house overlooking Woodvale Park, where they even vandalised the bushes. When I sat in the dentist's chair, I could see the tops of tall trees that had 'Tony Loves Sharon – True' carved into their boughs with the penknife I had won at the fairground in Millisle. Whenever I was trapped in that chair to have a hateful filling done, I would try to think of pleasant things to distract me from the pain. So, as the dentist drilled, I would look out of the window across the park and imagine Agnetha up a tree, singing 'Fernando'.

On the day my mother took me along to have my fangs checked, I sat in that same chair, dreading a diagnosis that would necessitate a cold sharp steel injection into the roof of my mouth. Fortunately, on this occasion, this was not to be the case. 'Your son requires orthodontic treatment as a matter of urgency, Mrs Macaulay,' said the dentist. 'I will arrange an appointment for him to see Mrs Osborne immediately.'

Within two weeks, I had my first visit to the orthodontist to arrange for a brace to be fitted, so that my vampire mouth could be pulled into shape. Mrs Osborne's orthodontic

surgery was located in one wing of her huge house up the
Malone Road, where all the wealthy people lived. On my
first appointment there, I was amazed to discover how the
real rich people lived.

Before this, the biggest house I had ever been in was a
four-bedroom detached house up the Antrim Road with
a double garage and an avocado bidet. That had been
impressive – but I had never been inside anything quite like
this before. There were rooms everywhere, and the walls
were covered with dark polished wood instead of woodchip
wallpaper. There was wood on the floor as well, instead
of shag pile. There were no fluorescent light tubes in the
kitchen. It was much more old-fashioned than our house,
more like the Rowings' place, but bigger and richer. They
hadn't knocked down the walls between the toilet and the
bathroom, neither had they removed any chimney breasts
to make more room and put in an electric fire. There were
no lava lamps or brown suede pouffes, even though I was
certain they could have afforded dozens of them. They had
very old-looking wooden furniture that you couldn't get on
hire purchase in Gillespie & Wilson on the Shankill, and they
had old chiming grandfather clocks and silver candlesticks
you couldn't buy in the Club Book.

All of this made me a little nervous. When we arrived
at Mrs Osborne's front door, I noticed it had stained-glass
windows like in a church. We were welcomed by a friendly
receptionist, and there was a woman with a mop bucket,
washing all the floors. 'Your granny used to clean for people
in big houses up here, y'know, son,' my mother explained.

Being surrounded by such opulence, I expected Mrs

Osborne to have a bun in her hair, and I assumed she would put us down with lots of 'ings', but when we met her she wasn't like that at all. Yes, she did talk like a lady on Radio Ulster, but she was very warm and friendly. I was wearing my BRA uniform, and I wondered if that was what made her so nice to me, but she seemed to be so genuine that she might even fix my fangs if she found out I was a paperboy with dirty hands from up the Shankill.

My mother accompanied me to Mrs Osborne's palace that day, and, because we were on the Malone Road, she spoke to the orthodontist in her Gloria Hunniford telephone voice. She attempted most of her 'ings' in such locations, even though she knew my father would have disapproved. 'Are you go-ing to be eat-ing some cucumber sandwiches on the lawn in the gard-ing ?!' Daddy would mock, when he suspected she was getting above her station. 'No son of mine will ever try to be something he's not!' he would say to me at the slightest hint of an emergent middle-class BRA accent.

The first visit to my orthodontist was all very pleasant and going very well.

'Yes, the boy will need a brace on his upper teeth for about twelve months,' advised a very professional Mrs Osborne.

'Will he have to wear the brace while he is eat-ing?' enquired my mother politely.

'No, he can take it out during meals. We will take an imprint of his teeth at the next appointment, but he will have to have two teeth extracted first,' she continued in a matter-of-fact manner.

Silence.

'Does he have to have some teeth tak-ing out?' asked my mother, with an unmistakable look of concern on her face.

'Yes, my dear. These two here,' replied Mrs Osborne pointing with her sharp steel instrument at my two condemned teeth.

Another pause.

I knew what my mother was thinking. I immediately deduced the source of her concern and her next question simply confirmed my conclusion.

'But our Tony has a bad heart, so he does, and Mr Pantridge at the Royal says that if he ever has to get a tooth out, he needs to go into hospital in case, well, just in case,' she said, while making the strange expression with her eyebrows she sometimes used to indicate to other adults that I wasn't supposed to be hearing something.

'Will he be all right?'

'This little chap will be just fine,' replied Mrs Osborne, clearly untroubled by the life-threatening situation she was forcing me into. I had never heard someone who wasn't English use the word 'chap' before. They always talked about 'chaps' in *The Two Ronnies* on BBC 1.

'I will arrange for the extraction to be carried out at the School of Dentistry in the Royal,' added Mrs Osborne.

I was in shock. I had lots of questions in my head. Was it a life-threatening operation? What are the average survival rates for boys with bad hearts getting teeth out?

I found I wanted to ask the question they always asked Dr McCoy in the sickbay in *Star Trek* in such dire circumstances: 'What are my chances, Bones?'

But here I was in a big house up the Malone Road under the authority of a posh lady who you just could never question, and so I didn't dare articulate my inquiries out loud. I quietly accepted my fate. My mother looked worried, but did not question either. It wasn't fair. Just when I had begun to accept that I had a future with a fully beating heart, now everything was up in the air again – and all for the sake of having teeth more like an Osmond than a vampire.

On the day of the operation, I was very nervous. When we arrived at the Royal, and I got my first whiff of disinfectant at the front door, I was more worried than the day of my Eleven Plus or the night I had to do a violin solo at the school concert. I spent what I knew could very well be my final hour sitting in the waiting area, reading an old copy of *Look-in* I found among a pile of well-thumbed *Woman's Owns*. I tried to read an article about why Alvin Stardust always wore a black leather glove on one hand, but I couldn't really concentrate.

As the nurse ushered me into the operating room, I was aware my days could be numbered. I said a prayer and did a deal with God: as I had asked Jesus into my heart on the bin at the caravan and been good livin' for years now, I in return asked if He would look after me and keep me out of Heaven for another wee while yet. But before I could finish the Lord's Prayer, they had knocked me out with gas.

Five minutes later, when I awoke, I was alive but minus two teeth. I was very drowsy and a little confused, and was sick once again over my Harrington jacket, but at least my bad heart was still going. I started to cry like a wee boy, and it was all very embarrassing as my mammy comforted me, but at least I had survived. I thought I had been knocked out for hours. It was like when the Russians put a drug in James Bond's drink and made him have hallucinations, before torturing him for secrets about big atom bombs. The whole day my mother had pretended it was all very routine, but now she also looked very relieved indeed. I would live to deliver the papers another day. And if I was very lucky and splashed on just enough Brut, I might still experience endless snogs with Sharon Burgess at the Westy Disco.

Now that the two teeth beside my incisors had been removed and it became clear that my bad heart was continuing to beat, I was able to return to Mrs Osborne, so that the process of bringing the rebellious fangs under control could be continued. I thought the trauma was over, but there was more pain and humiliation to come. Mrs Osborne took an imprint of my upper teeth with horrible putty that tasted like mud with toothpaste, and then she made a brace of plastic and wire especially for my mouth. I had looked forward to getting my brace, because it made you look grown-up, but as soon as I inserted it in my mouth for the first time I discovered an unforeseen problem – I couldn't speak properly! A brace gave you a speech impediment. Every 's' sound became a 'ssch'.

'How am I sschupposed to sschpeak with thissch thing in?' I complained to my mother.

'You'll just have to put up or shut up, love!' Mammy replied. 'You don't want to end up looking like Christopher Lee when you grow up. You'll never get no girls nor nathin' if you end up lookin' like a vampire.'

I practised hard to enunciate my words properly, but

in the end I had to accept that I would never be able to pronounce an 's' normally while wearing my brace. And so I had great difficulty with all the most important words in life, such as 'SSchowaddywaddy', 'sschex', 'Protesschtantsschs' and 'Catholicssch'.

This new handicap caused great upset in many different areas of my life. At home, my wee brother had great fun, repeatedly asking me the name of the spaceship in *Star Trek*. After my third attempt at '*SSchtarsschip Enterprissch*', I realised he was doing it on purpose.

At school, after our first performance of *The Adventures of Tom Sawyer and Huckleberry Finn*, I overheard our female Huck mimicking me to wee Thomas O'Hara. 'Hi Tom SSchawyer!' she said, before bursting into laughter. It was interesting that she never did this in front of me. Huck obviously didn't have the balls.

This was all very embarrassing, but when it started to affect my profession it was clearly becoming a much more serious problem. When collecting the paper money on a Friday night, for instance, I had great difficulty in communicating to Mrs Charlton with the Scottish accent who lived in No. 102 that she owed me £1.66. 'I dinnae ken what yer saying, love,' she repeated after several vain attempts on my part to communicate the detail of her weekly papers bill. In the end, I had to write it down. It all seemed so inconvenient, and yet I knew that I would have to persist though pain and embarrassment, otherwise I would grow up to look like the undead.

Sharon Burgess of course didn't have to get a brace.

Her teeth were perfect. They were white and straight and lovely, like Marie Osmond's. My sweetheart's pure teeth just made me want to kiss even more. Big Ruby at the caravan had taught me how to kiss properly in the sand dunes. It was a different type of kiss to any I had ever experienced before – nothing like the sort of kiss you would get from your granny at Christmas or from your Auntie Doris who was a lovely singer in Lambeg. No, this was real kissing. Big Ruby had said it was called a French kiss. I couldn't for the life of me understand the connection, because Big Ruby was from the Newtownards Road and had never even been to France. But she was very generous nonetheless, taking the chewing gum out of her mouth especially so as to show me how to use my tongue. She also told me that if you ran your fingers through the girl's hair when you kissed her, it meant you really loved her in your heart. My first real kiss with Big Ruby was pleasant enough, although it was slightly ruined when a cheeky breeze off the Irish Sea blew some sand in my mouth.

But I didn't fancy Big Ruby, so kissing her wasn't the real thing. It was a bit like learning how to score a goal in a football match on your big brother's Subbuteo set on the living-room floor, instead of scoring a real goal for Man United in the FA Cup Final at Wembley. My first real kiss had been with Sharon Burgess at the Westy Disco. I had persuaded my DJ dad to put on a slow song at just the right moment, after I had got Sharon up on the dance floor to do the Bump with me. As my father carefully faded the music into Donny Osmond, Sharon stayed up on the dance floor with me to slow dance to 'Puppy Love'. My bad heart fluttered a little as she put her arms around me and we danced. I ran my fingers through her hair, so I did.

As Sharon closed her eyes and held me tight around the waist that first time, I hoped that she was thinking of me and not Donny. But these days, after the disturbing revelations of the jumble sale, my greatest fear was that it was actually my big brother she longed to embrace on the dance floor of the Westy Disco.

# CHAPTER SEVENTEEN

## *musical distractions*

B-A-Y,

B-A-Y,

B-A-Y-C-I-T-Y,

With a R-O-L-L-E-R-S —

Bay City Rollers are the best!

Our day had come, so it had. We were a gaggle of excited teenagers in high-waisted parallels assembled at our neighbourhood bus stop at the top of the Shankill. Together we were waiting for a black taxi to take us down the Road into the much-abused city centre, so as to see the Bay City Rollers concert in the Ulster Hall. Bedecked in tartan from the berets on our heads to the Doc Martens on our toes, we were chanting Rollers' classics non-stop. It was unreal, like a dream come true.

In the excitement of getting all our tartan regalia in place, we had missed the bus into town and the next one wasn't due for ages — if it wasn't hijacked in the meantime. As the only pacifist paperboy in West Belfast, I had certain moral difficulties with using an illegal black taxi instead of the bus, because the taxi money would go to the paramilitaries — but this was an emergency. I justified my actions on this occasion with the thought that once the taxi driver had taken out a percentage for petrol and cigarettes from my 10p fare, there probably wouldn't be enough left to buy a whole bomb. I had waited for this day for months, and nothing, not even being a blessed peacemaker, was going to stop me from getting to the Ulster Hall in time to see the Scottish superstars perform their greatest hits right there in front of me.

I have to admit that I had rushed my paper round that day. I had been careless with too many gates and had leapt over a number of fences and hedges that were not approved for jumping. Even the fear of disciplinary procedures from Oul' Mac could not hold me back on this occasion. Every second was vital, and so I had to cut corners. I had intentionally skipped the final crucial stage of fully pushing the newspapers into expectant homes. Half the houses on the street had newspapers hanging out of their letterboxes. The semi-posted *Belfast Telegraphs* looked all droopy and forlorn, like Petra's tail when she ran away up the street after you kicked her for trying to have sex with your leg like a boy dog.

All the gang was there. My big brother was the leader of the pack, in black parallels and with only a subtle hint of tartan in the lining of his black Harrington jacket. He was a fan, but he was determined not to express too much adoration of the Rollers, in case it made him sound homo – and he was careful not to overdo it with the tartan accessories. If any of us got too enthusiastic, he would command us to 'Wise a bap!' and we would dutifully obey.

If my big brother was the godfather of the gang, then Heather Mateer was the godmother. Heather was the most mature: she was sixteen, with breasts, and leaving school soon. She had feathered hair, done at His n' Hers beside the Shankill graveyard, and she was wearing a long tweed coat over her white parallels with a tartan stripe up the side. (The same ones that had ripped at Corrymeela and which her ma had sewn back together again.) Heather was wearing the tweed coat just in case she got overexcited, because she knew if her parallels split again and we saw her knickers once more, we would laugh our heads off and she would be scundered in front of the whole of the Ulster Hall. She was also sporting five tartan scarves tied together which she had wrapped around her neck and flung over her shoulder: she looked like a tartan girl Doctor Who.

Heather had a bad Belfast habit of starting every sentence with the word 'like' for no apparent reason.

'Like, when's this bloody black taxi comin'?' she asked.

'Like, I hope my ma sewed these parallels tight enough,' she fretted.

'Like, I can't wait to see that lovely Les McKeown in the flesh!' she drooled.

Most of us talked this way at times, but Heather did it in every sentence. I noticed that fewer people at BRA began their sentences with 'like', so to fit in there, I had successfully tried to reduce my usage of the word. Like, I didn't want to sound as if I came from up the Shankill or anything.

Heather Mateer's best friend, Lynn McQuiston with the buck teeth, was there too. Lynn was the biggest Bay

City Rollers fan in the world. She had all their singles, and her bedroom wall was covered with so many Rollers posters that you couldn't even see the woodchip. Lynn was obsessed with the lead singer, Les McKeown. 'I just love Les, so I do,' she kept repeating as she gazed at a card with a picture of her idol which she had got free from a bubble-gum pack. Lynn knew his birthday and his height and the colour of his eyes and his favourite animal and everything. She wanted us to go straight to the stage door at the back of the Ulster Hall, where, she dreamed, she would meet Les and their relationship would begin: they would get married, and she would go on tour with him if he didn't want to come and live in the Shankill because of the Troubles and all. At least Lynn had thought things through.

Titch McCracken was there at the bus stop too, of course. He was wearing an old pair of white parallels almost up to his knees which he had clearly grown out of – even though he hadn't grown very much at all. I thought they looked disturbingly tight around the region of his jimmy joe. 'Like, them trousers must be cuttin' the willy off ye, wee lad!' said Heather Mateer sympathetically. Heather had a beautiful way with words.

Titch's mother must have put the said trousers in the wash with his purple jumper, because they were also slightly pink. 'What are ye doing in pink parallels, ya wee fruit?' my big brother felt compelled to ask.

Titch also had a tartan scarf attached to his wrist, but as he had tied it round his smoking hand, he kept getting ash on his tartan, leading me to fear that his scarf would meet the same sad fate as his cindered paperbag in the telephone

box. He was sharing drags of his cigarettes with Philip
Ferris, who didn't deserve to be there at all, in my view. He
had made no effort whatsoever: there was not so much as
a splash of tartan on the brown duffle coat he was wearing.
Even I knew a duffle coat was not appropriate attire for a
rock concert! Philip was more interested in playing five-a-
side football with the Boys' Brigade than anything remotely
musical.

'Like, could you not have borrowed a tartan scarf for the
night?' inquired Heather Mateer.

'Bay City ballicks!' Philip grunted in response.

Irene Maxwell was there too, smothered in every tartan
accessory she had ever seen in *Jackie*. This included a denim
and tartan Donny Osmond style beret, purple parallels with
tartan stripes and tartan waistband and tartan pocket flaps
and tartan turn-ups, as well as tartan scarves attached to
most of her limbs. Irene was also wearing an Eric Faulkner
T-shirt and a host of badges proclaiming 'I love Eric'. Her
brazen infidelity to David Cassidy that day was shocking.

'I wonder if Big Jaunty will be there the night?' she asked,
irritatingly.

'He liked the Bay City Rollers before he moved to
Bangor and he was lovely, so he was, and he looked like
David Cassidy, so he did,' she gushed.

I had to tune her out or she would potentially spoil the
whole evening.

The presence of Sharon Burgess, however, ensured that
the evening could not be spoiled. She wore a brown tank
top over a brown blouse with a big round brown collar, and
brown parallels with a tartan stripe down the side. Sharon

was a vision in brown. Of all the girls, her parallels went closest to her ankles, which only went to prove that she was the nicest girl there. She had got her mother to flick her brown hair like Farrah Fawcett-Majors especially for the occasion. She was lovely with her brown eyes, and she was my angel. She let me hold her hand at the bus stop without so much as a 'wise up, wee lad!' My big brother was paying no attention to her thus far, and it seemed to me that Sharon was most interested in Eric Faulkner anyway.

As for me, I was wearing my best green parallels from John Frazer's, with Macaulay tartan stripes fresh from Princes Street in Edinburgh, professionally sewn down the sides on my mother's sewing machine. I was also wearing my best brown-and-cream striped tank top and my Harrington jacket. I splashed some extra Brut all over it to mask any residual whiff of boke from my traumatic trip to get my teeth out and tomato sauce from the Geordie Best sausages at the jumble sale.

At last the black taxi arrived at the bus stop, and we all crammed inside. The smell of Brut aftershave and Charlie perfume was overwhelming. (Charlie was like Brut for girls, except they didn't need to splash it all over.) The black-taxi driver was an Elvis fan with UVF tattoos and a beer belly. His glasses had a brown tint that went ever darker as the evening sun came out.

'And where are yousens goin'?' he asked.

'We're goin' to see the Bay City Rollers at the Ulster Hall, and I just love Les, so I do,' answered Lynn McQuiston, oblivious to the intended irony of the question.

Ten minutes and dozens of choruses of 'We love you,

Rollers' later we were down the Shankill Road and in the town. Once we had emerged from the black taxi, my big brother expressed his disgust that we boys had been joining in the chants of 'We love you, Rollers'. He gave us a brief lecture, explaining that boys should refrain from singing along with anything that referred to loving the Rollers, because boys shouldn't sing about loving other boys, or everyone would think we were 'f\*\*kin' fruits'. And so henceforth, we clapped or stamped our feet aggressively along to any mantras that used the word 'love' in appreciation of our heroes, and we contented ourselves with shouting 'Yo!' manfully every so often instead of joining in with the singing.

As we arrived in Bedford Street, we were greeted by the queue outside the Ulster Hall – a seething mass of tartan and parallels, singing:

> Woody, Eric, Alan, Leslie and Derek –
> We love you, Rollers
> Rollers, we love you!

I had never seen such a large crowd on a Belfast street without the presence of petrol bombs. I was so enthralled that I joined in with the singing immediately – until my big brother kicked me in the shins and I remembered the Love Rule. The atmosphere was amazing.

We were about to join the end of the longest queue I had ever seen, when Lynn McQuiston reminded us of her plans to begin a relationship with Les McKeown at the stage door.

'Like, I don't even know where the stage door is,' said Heather.

'Wise a bap!' said my big brother.

'Ballicks!' said Philip Ferris, of course.

It was at this moment that my experience of the School of Music came in handy in a most unexpected way. I had played my violin in the back row of the second violins in the School of Music Orchestra concert in the Ulster Hall the previous year. It was such a big occasion that even Patrick Walsh had played in the orchestra that day, despite the fact that he generally said the Ulster Hall was just for Protestants. On the day itself, I had in fact nearly fallen off the stage, when I dropped my chin rest and one leg of my chair teetered perilously over the edge of the podium towards an audience that was heavy with gold jewelry and whispered 'ings'. Anyway, as a performing artiste, I had entered the Ulster Hall that day by the aforementioned stage door. So I knew exactly where the stage door was. It was in the next street at the back of the hall itself.

'Follow me!' I said triumphantly, much to my big brother's disgust. For once, I was the leader, and he would have to follow.

I led the gang down a side street of shops that were boarded up from the latest car bomb. In less than a minute there we were, standing at the stage door at the rear of the Ulster Hall. Amazingly, there was hardly anyone else there apart from a few other tartan-clad girls sobbing and screaming, and a couple of RUC men who were clearly more used to policing angry rioters than hysterical teenagers.

'They're already inside, so yousens may as well go back round and get into the queue, kids,' said one of the RUC men with a moustache when he saw us.

I turned around immediately to obediently return to our place in the queue.

'Houl' yer horses!' said my big brother. 'They're not here yet!' I was shocked at this remark. It had never occurred to me that the RUC would tell lies.

'Like, the peelers wouldn't still be here if the Rollers was already inside!' said Heather, excitedly.

'Oh my God, my Les is gonna be right here any minute nigh!' shrieked Lynn.

'Ballicks,' said Philip.

No sooner had he yet again demonstrated just how limited his vocabulary was than a long black limousine with the windows blacked out like a police car pulled up in front of us. What happened next was like a dream. It seemed to happen in slow motion, like the Six Million Dollar Man running. Right before our very eyes, five young men dressed in parallels and tartan emerged from the limousine in quick succession. Alan and Derek, the two brothers, got out first and escaped through the stage door before we had fully grasped the reality of what was happening in front of us. Eric Faulkner was next.

'Eric!!' screamed Irene Maxwell, as she ran forward and grabbed his jacket. It was like a sick woman touching Jesus in a story in Sunday school. Eric turned briefly and smiled at her. His face was mirrored in the T-shirt Irene was wearing. She fainted. As Titch McCracken and Sharon Burgess knelt down to see if she was all right, and before we had a chance to take all of this in, the real, live Les McKeown from off *Top of the Pops* was suddenly running straight past us.

'I loooove you Les!' screamed Lynn McQuiston

repeatedly, the tears streaming down her face onto her buck teeth, as she reached out and grabbed at a tuft of hair on the back of his head. Les just looked scared and kept running.

While the girls in our gang had known instinctively how to approach this situation – by screaming and attempting to touch their idols, the boys didn't know what to do. We didn't want to scream or touch our heroes, but we did want to make some more masculine kind of connection with them. So we did what came most naturally to us – we kicked them.

My big brother led the way, and just managed to land a boot on Les McKeown's backside, leaving a dirty boot print on the lead singer's white parallels. It was then that fate intervened once again in my favour. The last Roller to get out of the car was Woody the drummer, and I found myself standing right beside him. So what did I do? Did I ask him for his autograph? No – he was moving much too fast for such niceties. Did I shout, 'We love you Woody!'? Of course not – my big brother had forbidden such expressions. So I did what I knew best: I kicked him. In the heat of the moment, I abandoned my pacifist principles for the second time that day and expressed my adoration of a pop idol in the only way I knew how. I kicked him in the shins. Yes, I kicked Woody!

Once the Rollers were safely inside the Ulster Hall, we looked at each other in excited silence. We had seen all the Rollers in real life! We had screamed at them, touched them and kicked them. As we rejoined the queue, we relived those precious moments – something we would continue to do for the next six months afterwards.

'I touched Eric and he smiled at me and I fainted!' said Irene. 'I'll never wash my hand again!'

'I touched Les and he knows I love him and I think he loves me back,' said Lynn sadly, looking down in awe at a clump of Les's hair in her hand. 'I'll never wash my hand again!'

'I kicked yer man Les!' boasted my big brother. 'That'll harden him!'

'I kicked Woody!' I rejoined guiltily. 'I'll never, er … wash my foot again!'

Titch McCracken looked up at me, stubbed out his cigarette on the pavement and then followed it up by spitting contemptuously and rolling his eyes.

My heart was now beating very quickly with the excitement of it all. For a second I wondered if God was going to let my bad heart kill me before the beginning of the show – as a punishment for using violence on a pop star. But mercifully, He spared me and I got to see the whole concert in its full glory.

Once inside the historic building, the chants of 'We Love You, Rollers' were deafening. I had never heard so many girls screaming, even after a bomb, and neither had the Ulster Hall, I'm sure. We made our way to our prime seats, up in the balcony. Looking down on the stalls below, teeming with tartan teenagers, I felt slightly dizzy.

It seemed like we had to wait for ever for the concert to begin. The longer we waited, the more the tension grew and the more the screams intensified. I began to get fed up with all this stupid screaming and passed the time by counting the number of pipes on the big organ at the back of the stage.

It felt as if the whole crowd was about to explode, when suddenly the lights went out. At first I thought the Provos had blown up an electricity transformer again, but then I realised that this was what Miss Baron would have called 'dramatic effect'. One minute there was complete darkness and the next there were five spotlights on five figures. I recognised them of course from *Top of the Pops* and also from up close at the stage door. The Bay City Rollers were here, now. They were live! The screaming reached an even higher pitch. It was so piercing that I had to put my hands over my ears. The concert began. I couldn't actually hear the Rollers, what with all the screaming and with my ears covered. Heather, Irene, Lynn and even Sharon Burgess screamed and cried through the classic ballad 'Give a Little Love'. I put my arm round Sharon Burgess and she didn't tell me to wise up, but she wouldn't turn her lips towards me either, because that would have meant taking her eyes off Eric Faulkner.

Every so often, if the screams began to calm down, Les would turn his back to the audience and shake his bum. For some reason, this made the girls go wild, but every time he did it, I was sure I could see the boot mark from my big brother's Doc Martens on the backside of Les's white parallels. Philip Ferris watched carefully through every guitar solo, and kept accusing the Rollers of miming. We all sang along to 'Summer Love Sensation', and I noted that my big brother knew every word – even though he was supposed to be an Alice Cooper fan who hated teenyboppers. Meanwhile, Heather Mateer started to dance up too close to him, but he was playing it cool because he preferred girls who did gymnastics. I noted with some relief that Heather's flirtations with my big brother did not appear to be upsetting Sharon Burgess.

Woody sat behind the drums and didn't attempt any dancing, so I wasn't able to ascertain whether he had developed a limp due to my recent attack. He seemed to be able to step on the pedal of the bass drum okay, so I reassured myself that I had done no lasting damage to his shins or his musical career.

As the concert continued, the volume of the screaming and the pitch of the temperature in the Ulster Hall went ever upwards. The hall was full of the smell of the sweat and cigarettes and the spearmint chewing gum of a thousand teenagers. There was a powerful crescendo of hormones, heat and noise. We were happy, we were alive, and, for a few hours, we didn't think or care about homework or gunmen or bomb scares or there being no jobs.

'The Belfast crowd are the best audience in the world!' proclaimed Les between hits, and we loved him even more.

Of course it couldn't last for ever, and when at last it came to the final encore of 'Shang-a-Lang', the whole of the Ulster Hall erupted into a new level of frenzy. Unfortunately the crowds on the balcony surged forward so fast that the front panel of the balcony began to give way, as if it might fall on the fans below. There was a serious danger that Rollers fans from above might rain down upon the unsuspecting crowd below in the stalls.

Luckily, the security men noticed the impending disaster immediately and sprang into action. With the assistance of several RUC men with moustaches, they dutifully spent the last verse of 'Shang-a-Lang' clinging onto the front panel of the balcony with all their might. When the concert finally ended and we began to leave the Ulster Hall in our droves, the security men stayed where they were, holding onto the front of the balcony to stop it collapsing onto the rows below. They were sweating more than us.

Our gang had to walk home in the rain that night because there weren't enough black taxis for everyone – we clearly had overwhelmed the paramilitary public-transport system. We didn't care, though. We sang 'Shang-a-Lang' as we ran with the gang the whole way home up the Shankill. When I finally got into my bed that night, I kept waking up, trying to figure out what had been real and what had been a dream.

The next day at school, I swapped my usual grammar-school scarf with a tartan scarf, even though this was against the rules and it clearly didn't go with my duffle coat. When I arrived in the playground that morning, I noticed Ian, formerly of the TITS, standing against the wall sullenly reading his *NME*. I couldn't resist deliberately walking past him, whistling 'Shang-a-Lang' loudly and flaunting my tartan scarf. Ian pretended not to hear or see me, but I knew I had provoked a response when he aggressively turned the pages of the Status Quo feature he was reading and spat on the ground disgustedly. At that moment, Miss Baron was walking past and told him off for spitting in the playground. 'We are not hooligans at this school!' she scolded. 'We are civilised here.'

Ian got detention, and stuck a 'Kick Me' sign on the

back of my blazer with chewing gum at lunchtime for revenge. I drifted through every class that day in a daze, retaining even less knowledge than usual, apart from in French when the teacher nipped me under the arm until I got my verbs right.

However, when I picked up my forty-eight *Belfast Telegraphs* from Oul' Mac's van that night, I was shocked by the reports about the Bay City Rollers concert on their pages. Old men were saying that the Rollers fans were uncivilised hooligans, even worse than spitting schoolboys. Instead of rave reviews of the happiest night in Belfast for years, there were angry people claiming that teenagers at the pop-music concert in the Ulster Hall the previous night had vandalised the balcony. There were allegations that the concert had turned into a riot that could have ended in tragedy. There were cross baldy men demanding that there should be no more pop concerts in the Ulster Hall ever again, because we couldn't be trusted not to wreck it. This was unfair! We were being misrepresented. This was what John Hume called injustice.

I delivered my papers reluctantly and angrily that night. It felt like I was personally delivering untruths about myself to my own customers. It was the first time ever that I had hated doing my papers. I began to wonder if there were other career opportunities that I could pursue in the future. As I wandered home that night humming 'Give a Little Love', I considered my potential for delivering milk or bread, neither of which could tell lies. Or perhaps becoming an international spy like James Bond, or an astronaut who got lost in an anomaly in time and space. I was growing up, so I was.

# CHAPTER EIGHTEEN

## *across the walls*

I hated fences, so I did. They made life very difficult for a paperboy. The more my customers erected fences between each other, the more walking, running and jumping I had to do. This was particularly problematic and painful on a Friday night, when my Doc Martens were concealing coins from hoods and robbers.

There were four main types of fence: wire fences, hedges, wooden fences and walls. Wire fences were the easiest to negotiate, because there was usually a convenient hole in which to stick your foot for support as you clambered over to next door. However, if you weren't careful, this foothold could bend permanently into the shape of your boot. A customer could become suspicious and peek out through their net curtains to try to catch you red-footed and tell you to stop being such a 'lazy wee hallion' or else they would tell Oul' Mac.

Hedges were the next easiest to get over, because most would usually have sufficiently sturdy inner foliage to support the slight weight of a paperboy as you scaled their heights en route to the house next door. However, if you started to make a noticeable gap in the hedge, there were similar dangers of getting caught as with wire fences. The only difference was that at least with hedges there was the possibility that fresh leaves might eventually grow over your misdemeanours. I found I also had to face certain moral dilemmas with hedges. At some times of the year, stamping on the leaves would risk squashing many caterpillars underfoot – and as the only pacifist paperboy in West Belfast, I did not want to be responsible for the extermination of any of God's wee creatures.

Wooden fences were more of a hazard for two reasons. First of all, they were generally covered in rough sharp shards of wood that would stab your hands as you gripped on to jump over. You would end up with wee scalps in your fingers that got all infected and swollen so you couldn't practise your violin, and your daddy would have to poke the wee scalps out with a sharp needle, and you would have to try hard not to cry, because you were too big for crying by this time. The second problem was that most wooden fences up the Shankill were very cheap and fragile and couldn't support the weight of even a small paperboy, especially if it had been years since they had been painted to stop them from rotting. After several incidents where I caused damage that I managed to blame on Petra chasing Mrs Grant's pussy, I avoided any further attempts to put boot to wood.

The biggest challenge of all for a paperboy like myself was the brick or concrete wall. If such walls weren't too high, they were quite easy to jump over or sit on and swing over, but if they were very high, you had no other option but to walk around them. However, if they were walls of medium height which you thought might be easily scalable, you might make a serious misjudgement and end up colliding with hard and rough red brick, tearing your parallels, scraping your knees and elbows and maybe even ending up in the Royal for stitches.

Of course some of my customers had no fence at all, or just a little low row of flowers dividing them from their next-door neighbours. They always seemed to be the friendliest or poorest of my customers. They either didn't want to be separated from their neighbours or they couldn't afford to be. On the other hand, I noticed that for some of my customers, fences were very important indeed. They tended to be the rudest or the richest of my clientele or the ones with big snarling dogs. Mr Black from No. 13 had high fences on either side of his house. Of course he had greyhounds, but they couldn't jump that high, so I knew he just didn't want anybody next or near to him. 'Good fences make good neighbours!' he would proclaim.

I don't think Mr Black was aware that he was quoting from a Robert Frost poem I was studying in my English class. I was certain he had no idea that the line he was quoting was supposed to be what my English teacher called 'an ironic poetic device'. I began to notice that the people who made comments like 'good fences make good neighbours' always seemed to be the sort of characters you really wouldn't want to live beside anyway.

Another two such customers of mine, the Morrisons and the Smiths, had a real fence war going on. It started out as just one small wire fence between the two houses. Then the Morrisons put up a new wire fence without consulting the Smiths. So the Smiths put up another, higher wire fence on their property. These fences were starting to look like the ones on Colditz that I used to watch on BBC 1. In response, the Morrisons added a wooden fence that was even taller than their neighbours' higher wire fence. Then the Smiths vengefully erected a six-foot wall with a six-foot wooden fence on top of it. In the end, neither side were getting any sun on their nasturtium borders any more.

All this reminded me again of that poem from English class, which said, 'Something there is that doesn't love a wall.' Maybe Robert Frost had been a paperboy too. I always enjoyed studying poems about war and walls much more than doing Shakespeare, because at least these poems were about ordinary everyday life that I could relate to.

Of course, there were even bigger walls in the city than those between my customers. In fact, we were brilliant at walls in Belfast – they were going up everywhere, higher and higher, all around me. For every inch that I grew, the walls surrounding me got six foot higher. Ever since the start of the Troubles, they had been putting walls up between Protestant and Catholic streets to stop us killing each other. Of course, it didn't work because ever since they built them we had been slaughtering each other even more. Most people on both sides, however, thought that the walls between us were a good idea, and it wasn't very often Catholics and Protestants agreed on anything. I suppose the walls made me feel safer because they helped me believe that it would be harder for the other side to get at me. When the walls were put up, you couldn't see the other side any more and they couldn't see you, and that was better for everybody. And if you wanted to show the other side how much you hated them, at least you had an obvious place to go to, to throw stones and bricks over at them. You didn't have to look at exactly what damage you had done to the other side, but at least you could be pretty sure you had hurt them.

Everyone called them 'peace walls', which I thought was funny, but not funny ha-ha. It was very strange, I thought, to call these walls peace walls, because there hadn't been any of them before the Troubles, when we had peace. The parts of Belfast that had the most peace didn't have peace walls. And the places in the city with the biggest peace walls were the streets where Catholics and Protestants had lived together previously, before they started burning each other out – like the Springfield Road, where my father grew up and where my other granny had got out just in time.

Everywhere else in the world that had peace didn't have peace walls. However, in history class I learned about another big wall in another city: the Berlin Wall, which separated the goodies in West Germany from the baddies in East Germany. (Although my granny continued to insist that all Germans were still baddies.) The Berlin Wall was, as far as I could tell, a huge curtain made of iron and apparently it was going to be there for ever. Not like our peace walls in Belfast, which were only going to be here until the Troubles were over.

I wanted the Troubles to be over tomorrow because they were all I could ever remember. I hated all the fighting and killing more than I hated any Catholics or even the IRA. I thought that it probably didn't matter when you got killed whether the ground around your coffin was Irish or British muck. Everyone said you could never trust the other side. Apparently there were actually some good ones, but, generally speaking, you couldn't trust them. Catholics were all supposed to support the IRA and wanted to kill us for a United Ireland. So we had to defend ourselves to stay British, because that was the most important thing in the whole world. I was never quite so sure about all of this. I knew that all the Catholics on the other side of the peace wall had too many children and did Irish dancing, but I couldn't accept that they all wanted me dead. I was curious as to what they were really like over there. I had so many questions. Did they learn at their church too that we were all going to Hell? Did they want to put us all on the Larne–Stranraer ferry back to Scotland? Did they really believe we were all rich? Were their paramilitaries full of wee hard men that liked to boss everyone around, like ours were?

I was curious about everyday life on the other side of our Peace Wall too. I wondered if they had paperboys over there as well, and, if so, did the Provos allow them to deliver the *Ulsters* on a Saturday night? Maybe there were wee lads over there too with bad hearts and braces who were worried that Sinead O'Burgess was falling in love with their big brother (who was brilliant at Gaelic football). Maybe the same mothers that we could hear banging their bin lids every August on the anniversary of Internment also sewed dresses for posh ladies and ordered toys for Christmas from the Great Universal Club Book (even though it was posted from England).

My father questioned divisions between working-class people just as much as he questioned the existence of God. He hated the peace walls as much as I hated the fences between my customers. They had knocked down Lanark

Street, where his family came from, and put up a peace wall instead. My Da was definitely in the minority on the Shankill.

One summer evening in July, as I was returning home from finishing a particularly sweaty paper round, I came across my father arguing over the gate with Mrs Piper. She was wearing her usual black cardigan that never quite covered both breasts, even though she was constantly trying to pull either side across them.

'We need them walls til go up a quare bit higher yet,' Mrs Piper was explaining. 'Them Fenians is still gettin' petrol bombs over. And we need more gates on the roads too, so we can close them at night so as to keep them out.'

My father looked exasperated. He was never very good at hiding his exasperation, and so I always knew right away when I was in trouble.

'All I ever hear yousens sayin' is we need more walls put up to keep the other side out. Did you never think that it might be our side that's bein' walled in?' he asked.

Mrs Piper had clearly never thought of it this way before. She vainly attempted to pull her cardigan across her generous bosom once more, only now with great indignation.

'Well, if you don't agree the walls should go up higher, then you're just supportin' the IRA!' was her predictable reply.

This was always the response when you disagreed with Mrs Piper. My father's questioning the raising of the peace walls would now be added to a long list of errors that would support the suspicion that you sympathised with the IRA, and this was the ultimate sin, of course. An even worse sin than a mum running off with a soldier or a man being a homo. In the past, Mrs Piper had been known to assert that you supported the IRA if you didn't like Paisley or Orange bands, or if you did like Dana or Mother Teresa.

I know my father had stood up to this sort of thing before. He had a mind of his own. In his job as a foreman in the foundry he had once got a death threat wrapped around a bullet that had been placed in his locker, supposedly for giving a Catholic a job, instead of a Protestant. One day, Daddy had a blazing row in the middle of the street with a famous television reporter who he had observed giving money to children to throw stones at the soldiers, for the camera. He never forgave this. Every time the same journalist came on the news, reporting from some other war zone in another part of world, our family knew it was my father's cue to jump out of his chair and shout at the TV, 'There's that English bastard that paid the kids to throw stones at the soldiers!'

Of course, sometimes Daddy had to cooperate with the powers that be for the greater good. So, on one occasion, he was prepared to enter into negotiations with the UDA to get the Westy Disco gear back when it had been stolen during a heist on the Presbyterian church storeroom. It was the lesser of two evils.

'Your father's a very clever man,' affirmed my mother when these negotiations proved successful. He managed to get everything back, apart from a few Elvis singles.

One summer's day in 1977, I went up the fields again and looked down on Belfast as usual. I could see the peace walls snaking along the roads between neighbours all over my part of the city. There seemed to be more and more of them, and they seemed to be getting higher and higher by the day.

I thought again about my Robert Frost poem in English: 'Something there is that doesn't love a wall ...' I wondered about who was being walled out and who was being walled in. I speculated as to whether the peace walls would end up being here for ever, like the Berlin Wall. I imagined travelling through time to the future in the TARDIS with the Doctor, and landing up the fields above Belfast in the year 2000. Oul' Mac was being kept alive by a computer and his van was now all silver and space age, and it flew up and down the Shankill. The papers were being delivered by a robot paperboy. The Troubles were over long ago, and Protestants and Catholics went to the same schools together and played football together and lived in the same streets again, and the peace walls had all been torn down for ever. I was a dreamer, so I was.

# CHAPTER NINETEEN

## *winners*

The day of the Lord Mayor's Show had finally arrived. Our eagerness in anticipating this event was second only to the excitement that had led up to the day of the now legendary Bay City Rollers concert in the Ulster Hall. In spite of my ongoing concerns about Sharon Burgess and the allegations of the wee millie that Sharon fancied my big brother, today I was consumed with hope for a great victory for the members of the Westy Disco.

The Lord Mayor's Show was an annual event, with a big parade through the centre of Belfast past all the bombed-out shops and the City Hall. Hundreds of people came out onto the streets to watch all the colourful floats, and there was music and dancing, as well as prizes for the best entries, and no rioting. It was a bit like the parade on the Twelfth of July, except there were fewer flags and less drink, but more girls and Catholics.

This was not the first time that the members of the Westy Disco had entered a float for the Lord Mayor's Show. The previous year, we had dressed up as *The Wombles* for our float, and we had been awarded a 'Highly Commended' rosette for our efforts. My mother and Auntie Emma had spent weeks making Womble suits from old sacks and cotton wool. We had all dressed up and got onto the back of a lorry to sing 'Remember You're a Womble' around the streets of

Belfast. I had been given the part of Tobermory, which I thoroughly enjoyed – until, after hours of singing and dancing, my Womble suit got very hot and itchy. I endured this unpleasantness by imagining that I was an actor inside a Dalek on *Doctor Who* – as opposed to a boy inside a sack on the back of a lorry in Belfast. In spite of all the discomfort, it had been the best time ever. Children had waved and cheered at us all day long, and there had been a photograph of us in the *Belfast Telegraphs* I delivered. The whole carnival experience had left us hungry for more.

When Uncle Henry had got the letter inviting youth clubs to enter this current year's Lord Mayor's Show, he immediately brought it to the attention of the whole of the Westy Disco, during a short lull between Boney M and the Brotherhood of Man, and all those consulted were unanimous. We definitely wanted to enter the competition once again – but this year we were far too grown-up and cool to be Wombles. This year, we wanted to enter a float as the Bay City Rollers! We had to come up with a colourful banner that reflected the theme of the show, which was 'Rebuilding Belfast'. So my father came up with the slogan: 'BCR: Build, Construct, Renew'. My da was a very clever man, you know.

We soon got to work with all the preparations. It was a lot easier this year, because most of us dressed like the Rollers anyway, so there was no need to make special costumes for us. Our major task was building and painting a stage and banners to put on the back of the lorry. We used paint that my father had borrowed from the foundry and some wooden panels someone said had fallen off the back of another lorry. Belfast's emporium of fashion, John Frazer's, kindly donated sacks of tartan fabric fragments, and we painted and hammered and sewed until our creation was complete.

On the day of the show, our float was resplendent in tartan and packed full of tartan-clad teenagers in parallels on an unstable stage, singing Rollers songs at the tops of our voices. Five very lucky members of the Westy Disco had been chosen to be the Rollers themselves. Unfortunately I was passed over, just in case, following my starring role as a Womble the previous year, anybody thought my parents were guilty of favouritism. This was outrageous, I felt, because I would have made a far better Alan than Philip Ferris, who just kept saying as per usual that everything was 'ballicks'. Heather Mateer, with breasts, was chosen to be Les McKeown and Irene Maxwell was Derek. I thought this was even more perverted than Patricia Thompson's recent triumph on the stage at BRA as Huckleberry Finn, and I was amazed that Reverend Lowe did not even attempt to intervene. Worse still, Titch McCracken was picked to be Woody and I was so jealous I had an urge to kick him. (It had never occurred to me that I might ever want to kick Woody again.) But I relented when I saw wee Titch on the day, still wearing his too-tight pinkish parallels, as I assumed he would be in enough pain already without an assault on his shins by the only pacifist paperboy in West Belfast.

However, apart from my righteous anger regarding these two major injustices, I had been looking forward to this year's Lord Mayor's Show to the extent that I had almost forgotten the poisoned words of the wee millie about Sharon Burgess and my big brother. Sharon Burgess was a dancer in the Rollerettes, and my big brother was Eric Faulkner on guitar – I had been keeping a close eye on them, like 007 trying to catch out a double agent, but as far as I could tell there was still no spark between them.

On the day itself, we were brilliant! My father had rigged up the turntable and speakers from the Westy Disco on the back of the lorry and had somehow plugged them into the engine battery, and so the Rollers were blasting out up and down Royal Avenue and all around the City Hall. I had taken out my brace and left it at home because I knew I would otherwise have great trouble pronouncing the lyrics of 'Summer Love Sensation'. The crowds were smaller than the previous year, in case there were car bombs, but those who were there cheered and waved at us, especially all the teenagers in parallels.

It was amazing! We sang 'Shang-a-Lang' and 'Bye Bye, Baby' a million times until our throats were hoarse, and we waved our tartan scarves until our arms were aching. It was a Saturday, and I had the *Belly Telly* and the *Ulsters* to deliver that night, so I alone had to be careful to pace myself to ensure I would have sufficient energy left to carry out my professional duties later on.

After we had encircled the City Hall, we went with all the other floats up to the Lagan Embankment, where everyone parked in long rows to wait to be judged by the Lord Mayor and ladies in hats who were full of eager 'ings'. This stop was timed to coincide with lunchtime, so that everyone could get off their lorries, go to the toilets and have a pastie supper and juice from a wee chip van, before doing their very best performance for the judges. Last year we had been highly commended Wombles, but this year we were determined to be winning Rollers.

Once our lorry was parked on the banks of the Lagan, we also had the opportunity to dismount and check out the competition. You couldn't see the other floats during the parade, because they were either in front of you or behind you, but once the lorries were all parked together beside the river, you could walk up and down and assess your biggest rivals. We strolled up and down, admiring all the big fancy floats made of polystyrene advertising banks and businesses, but it was the other youth clubs in our category that we were most interested in. There weren't very many youth-club entries in the Lord Mayor's Show because young people weren't allowed out much in the Troubles – so we were in a very strong position.

Heather Mateer, obviously still on a high from being Les McKeown, finished her pastie supper first and grabbed my big brother by the tartan scarf, saying, 'C'mon and see who we have til beat this year!' My big brother went along with Heather without question, and I duly noted that this did not appear to cause any upset to Sharon Burgess. Irene Maxwell followed close behind the others, tartan scarves trailing from every limb.

'Heather Mateer fancies him, ya know,' I said slyly to Sharon, 'but he's only interested in Man United and girls that do gymnastics, so he is.'

There was no discernible response to the trap I had set. Sharon Burgess just continued dipping her last few chips into the residue of salt and vinegar on last night's *Belfast Telegraph*.

Me and Sharon would follow shortly, but we had to wait around for Titch because he had spilled brown sauce from his pastie supper on his pinkish parallels. A crowd of wee lads dressed as pirates on a float from the Shore Road had immediately pointed at his trousers and started shouting, 'Bay Shitty Rollers!' I had never seen Titch looking so scundered as he ran away to look for a toilet where he could try and clean up his trousers before the judging commenced. A few minutes later, Titch emerged from the crowd, all traces of the brown sauce removed from his parallels. However, he had used so much water to clean off the stains that now his trousers had a huge wet patch in all the wrong places! The pirates from the Shore Road reappeared from the crowd straight away of course; this time they pointed at Titch, shouting, 'Bay Pissy Rollers!' Poor Titch was so humiliated that he ran over and grabbed one of the pirates and told him that if he didn't shut up, he would kick him so hard he would be 'floating up the f**kin' Lagan in a bubble'. Then, just as this drama was unfolding in front of us, Heather Mateer arrived back on the scene, out of breath and bearing tidings of great import.

'We're up against the Belfast Girls' Gymnastics Club!' she screamed, 'and they're miles better than us, and your big brother loves them and ... you'll never guess who is doing DJ for them!'

'Where are they?' shouted Sharon.

'Follow me!' screamed Heather, jumping up and down excitedly. She was once again in severe danger of splitting her parallels. This could be even more embarrassing than the last time for her, because she still had to be Les McKeown up on a lorry in front of the Lord Mayor.

We all ran along the Lagan Embankment for ages, knocking over a wee girl's poke and tripping over several Petra-like labradors. Eventually we arrived at the site of the very impressive float of the Girls' Gymnastics Club. My big brother and Irene Maxwell were standing transfixed, gazing at the wonderful sight before them. I noticed, however, that they were looking in slightly different directions. The gymnastics girls were wearing sky-blue leotards and were dancing gracefully with ribbons and hoops to Demis Roussos and 'Dancing Queen'. It was truly international! My big brother was almost drooling. It was pathetic. He was watching the gymnasts even more closely than he would have watched a football match with Man United. He had never seen so many gymnastics girls in one place before. I have to admit, it soon got my attention too. It was like watching a mini *Miss World*, only on a lorry in Belfast.

I was beginning to enjoy the fact that there was one gorgeous wee girl that looked a bit like Farrah Fawcett-Majors – when suddenly I remembered that I was standing beside my girlfriend! I turned to Sharon quickly to pretend I had no interest whatsoever in the third gymnast on the left at the front, and I noticed she was looking upset all of a sudden. She wasn't paying any attention to me or the gymnastics girls, however. Sharon was staring at my big brother, and I could see jealousy written all over her face. Her lower lip was quivering, like when she had failed her

Eleven Plus, but this was even more serious. This was the sign I had been watching for but dreading. My girlfriend was clearly upset to see my big brother fancying so many gymnastics girls, because she fancied him herself even more!

Sharon spat out her chewing gum like a real millie and said, 'You'd think none of youse wee lads had ever seen a wee girl in a leotard before!'

Then Titch McCracken announced the devastating truth, 'You're just jealous, wee girl. Everybody's saying you fancy Tony's big brother and he doesn't fancy you back!'

I looked at Sharon sadly, while Titch looked at me sheepishly. Sharon looked away guiltily, but my big brother just kept looking at the gymnastics girls lustfully.

The truth was out! I was ragin'! I immediately regretted all the tip money I had spent on 'Love Is' cards for my girlfriend. I kicked myself for being so stupid and buying her Donny Osmond pyjamas for Christmas from the Club Book. I still had another ten weeks at 39p to pay!

'What's eatin' you, wee girl?' I asked sensitively.

'Wha?' Sharon replied, as if I had interrupted a dream.

'What's the matter?' I repeated.

'Ach nathin'!' she said stroppily. 'Leave me alone, wee lad!' she shouted and walked off towards the Westy Disco lorry all on her own. I let her go.

'You only went out with Tony to get near his big brother, ya wee millie!' Titch called after Sharon.

'Shut you up, Titch, ya wee glipe,' she shot back. 'You can fancy two people at the same time, ya know!'

I knew this was true. I fancied Agnetha and Farrah Fawcett-Majors at the same time. But this was different. It made my bad heart feel sore.

I had never seen Sharon Burgess like this before. She had never once been nasty to me before, even when I had pinched her bum the night we went to the Stadium Cinema to see *Jaws* and she had screamed louder at me than at the shark. But I wasn't stupid. Maybe the wee millie girl at the jumble sale had been exaggerating, but I now knew for certain that Sharon Burgess fancied my big brother! It wasn't fair, because she was lovely and I wanted her to be my own personal Olivia Newton-John. And my big brother preferred football to girls, and he preferred girls that did gymnastics anyway! It would never be the same between Sharon Burgess and me after that day. Our relationship was doomed. I accepted that we were not destined to be a for ever couple, like Agnetha and Björn from ABBA, or Princess Anne and Captain Mark Philips. It was over.

Then, just when I thought the day could not possibly get any worse, I noticed who Irene Maxwell was staring at so intently. Standing at the very front of the Belfast Girls' Gymnastics Club float, arrogantly doing DJ – with a dozen gymnasts in leotards looking up at him longingly – was no other than Trevor bloody Johnston. I thought he was supposed to be in Bangor!

'Oh my God!' shrieked Irene Maxwell. 'Look!! It's Big Jaunty and he's still as lovely as ever, so he is, and he still looks like David Cassidy, so he does!'

I suddenly had an urge to hijack this lorry and drive it into the river Lagan, where Trevor would get electrocuted by his microphone cable, after which I would remember I was a pacifist and do mouth-to-mouth resuscitation on all the pretty gymnastics girls.

''Bout ye, Jaunty!' shouted my big brother.

''Bout ye!' Trevor replied, proudly surveying his harem.

'D'ya need a hand?' asked my big brother, with uncharacteristic helpfulness.

It was unbelievable! Within minutes my big brother had become a love rival, and now here he was, helping out on a rival float with a rival paperboy. I wanted to shout out something damning like, 'How's your asthma, Trevor?!' or, 'What's it like, visiting your da in the Maze?!' I was torn, because I knew deep down that Jesus in my heart would not want me to be so nasty – but the Devil on my shoulder just wanted to see the reaction on the faces of the adoring gymnasts. However, before I even got the chance to do anything impulsive that I might have regretted later, Heather Mateer kept things moving along once again. 'C'mon, they're judgin' our float next!' she shouted.

We had to dash back along the Lagan Embankment at full speed. (This time we knocked a wee boy off his roller skates and spilled a pensioner's tea from her Thermos flask onto her knee.) We just made it.

Heather Mateer leapt up onto the stage first, because she knew we couldn't start without a Les McKeown. Inevitably, her parallels split once more, and she had to swiftly tie an extra tartan scarf around her waist, so the Lord Mayor couldn't see her knickers. Titch and Irene and me and my big brother were the last ones back onto the lorry, just as the Lord Mayor and the ladies with hats arrived, smiling appreciatively. My father pressed the button, and we were on. We sang and danced our hearts out in our efforts to bring a prize back to the Shankill. We did our very best, and, although the judges didn't look like they had bought too many Bay City Rollers singles recently, I was sure I could just about hear some very encouraging 'ings' over the music. As 'Bye Bye, Baby' blasted out, Titch McCracken looked at me, then at Sharon Burgess, and then at Eric Faulkner, and shook his head. Once again, I wanted to kick Woody.

As soon as all the judging was complete, the Lord Mayor and the ladies in hats walked along the Embankment once again, this time with huge rosettes to attach to the winners' lorries. If they walked past your lorry, it meant you hadn't won anything – but if they stopped at your float, it was a clear indication that you had won a prize.

We waited on our float with bated breath. It was a tense moment, like when the bomb-disposal unit was checking a suspect device. Some people couldn't handle the pressure. Philip Ferris told Heather Mateer that her Les McKeown performance had been 'ballicks', at which Heather flew into a rage, pulling his hair and kicking him between the legs. 'No, that's yer ballicks!' she screamed.

Philip Ferris ended up on the floor of the lorry clutching his groin, but no one went to help him. Heather Mateer's parallels were further split by the kicking action and she had to tie another two scarves around her waist, because you could nearly see her bum now. Titch McCracken kept taking wee sly peeks.

Just as this scuffle was breaking out, the Lord Mayor and the ladies with hats were approaching again. I could hear their 'ings' getting closer. Would they stop? Were we winners? Were we losers? Were we brilliant? Or just a lot of dirt from up the Shankill who even had a fight at the Lord Mayor's Show?

The judges stopped beside our lorry. The teenage population of Upper Shankill held its chewing-gum-flavoured breath. There was silence. Everything was completely still, apart from all the tartan scarves blowing gently in the breeze. Then, as if in slow motion, like the Bionic Woman, one of the ladies in hats lifted a large rosette and firmly attached it to the front of our lorry!

The rosette read: 'Winner – Second Prize. Highly Commended'.

'Winner!' shouted my father.

'Yooooo!' we screamed at the top of our voices.

We cheered and shouted, and then broke out into a spontaneous and never-ending encore of the Rollers' greatest hits. The Lord Mayor smiled, but the ladies in hats stepped back, looking a little nervous, as if they had just stroked a dog that had growled at them.

Within minutes, the engine of our lorry had started up again, and we began our victory parade back into town. As we turned onto the Ormeau Road where they made bread in the big bakery, we passed the Belfast Gymnastics Club float. My big brother and Irene Maxwell were once again distracted from their own performances by the performance of the others, and so, for a few minutes, we had no Derek or Eric in our Bay City Rollers. I caught a glimpse again of Sharon Burgess checking out my brother's attraction to the gymnasts. She had no chance! As I looked back in disgust towards the rival float, I noticed that they also had a rosette on the front of their lorry. This one said 'Winner – First Prize'.

It wasn't fair!

However, once our rivals were out of sight, they were very much out of mind. As we arrived back in the city centre, we prepared for our mighty victory parade back home, up the Shankill Road.

As we drove past Unity Flats, where the IRA lived, even Catholic teenagers cheered out their windows at us and nobody threw any bottles or bricks at all. Then we turned up the Shankill itself. As our lorry trundled up the Road towards the Black Mountain, gangs of tartan-clad teenagers began to follow us, in the same way they would have followed bands on the Twelfth of July. My father turned the speakers up full blast as we continued our victory parade from Lower Shankill to Upper Shankill. Women with prams stopped beside burnt-out pubs and smiled and pointed at us for their wee children. All my worries about bad hearts and cheating girlfriends and exams and bullets and hoods and robbers were a million miles away now.

Everyone was laughing and cheering and applauding us as we made our way up the Road. Oul' Mac even stopped his van and got out, standing with his hands on his hips, as if watching an alien spaceship landing. I'm sure he was even smiling with a couple of teeth. We didn't stop singing for the whole length of the Road, not even when the lorry passed over the security ramps and we had to hold on tight, in case we fell over in our platforms. A Saracen full of soldiers stopped, and they all got out and smiled and cheered with English accents. All the teenagers that were following us on the road sang along with us, even a few skinheads, and they weren't even drunk.

We were happy! We were young and alive and brilliant! We were winners! Well, Second Prize: Highly Commended. We sang 'Shang-a-Lang' as the gangs ran after us the whole way up to the top of the Shankill. We were Belfast kids! We weren't wee hooligans or thugs or terrorists! We didn't care what the rest of the world thought of us. We were proud Shankill kids! We weren't dirt! We were winners!

The following Monday at school I told everyone at BRA about our great victory, but most people weren't very interested, because apparently there had been some big rugby match on the same day. I had another argument in the playground with Ian, formerly of the TITS. He said that if he was going to dress up like an eejit in the Lord Mayor's Show, it would only be for a serious rock band, like Status Quo. I told Ian where he could stick his *NME*. Thomas O'Hara was the only person who had actually been there and had watched part of our float's victory parade past the City Hall. His da had taken a picture of our lorry with his Polaroid camera, and Thomas passed it round in Chemistry. Judy Carlton seemed very impressed, which pleased me greatly, now that it was becoming a case of 'Knowing Me, Knowing You' with Sharon Burgess.

That Monday evening, I delivered my papers more carefully than ever. There was a photograph of our Bay City

Rollers float in the Lord Mayor's Show in the centre of one of the inside pages. I utilised all my professional skills to gently fold each newspaper in a way that ensured our picture was never creased as I delivered the news of our great triumph through my customer's letterboxes. I was very proud. I was a winner, so I was.

# CHAPTER TWENTY

## *the last round*

By late 1977, the world was changing. Everything was in full colour now – the days of black and white were just a distant memory. Thankfully, Donny Osmond had been dumped by most wee girls and David Cassidy had simply disappeared. Sadly, it really was 'Bye Bye, Baby' for the Bay City Rollers, because now it was clear that ABBA reigned supreme. Meanwhile, at school, Ian, formerly of the TITS, was going on about some new thing in the *NME* called 'punk'. He was predicting that punk would hit the teenyboppers so hard that ABBA would be forgotten forever.

Irene Maxwell was getting very excited about a new film that was coming soon, with disco dancing and music by a group from the sixties called the Bee Gees. It sounded rubbish to me. I was more interested in news about a truly amazing movie that was about to be released. Apparently it was called *Star Wars*, and the clips I had seen on *John Craven's Newsround* made *Doctor Who* look wobbly.

Although I had never imagined it would ever happen, parallels were actually going out of fashion so fast that you could get a pair for 99p in the bargain bucket in John Frazer's. Only the biggest hard men and millies were still buying them. (Titch McCracken bought two pairs.)

Northern Ireland, though, was just the same – them and us, and killing and blame. I was six inches taller and the peace walls were twenty feet higher. It was harder than ever to be the only pacifist paperboy in West Belfast when the hatred ruled everything. It was becoming clear that the Troubles would be for ever, so I realised I would either have to get used to it or get out of it. I couldn't get out of it, so I would just have to get used to it.

By now, I had delivered thousands of papers, and my paperbag was deepest black in hue. Oul' Mac was a little older and a little yellower, but he had invested in a brand-new Ford Transit van. This was twentieth-century newspaper delivery. My employer had his new vehicle painted yellow, of course. After several months of gathering 'Wash Me' graffiti in its deepening dirt, it started to look exactly like the old van. This was Belfast after all, hard-wired to resist any apparent change.

I was changing, however. My fangs had been brought under control, and I no longer had the appearance of a bloodsucking monster. My brace was binned. Sources of distraction from my paper round were growing all the time. Schoolwork was harder, and homeworks were heavier. I now had GCEs looming, and they were like ten Eleven Pluses in a row. After-school clubs and new school friends from North Belfast were drawing me away from the streets of the Upper Shankill more and more. I stopped going to the Westy Disco every week, and on some Saturday nights I would visit friends' homes on the Antrim Road and in posh Glengormley. These were families who lived in chalet bungalows and went to Spain for their holidays. They had never been to a caravan in Millisle and their living rooms showed no trace of woodchip.

When I set out as a paperboy, my dreams were of being the Doctor with a TARDIS and a long scarf, fighting intergalactic battles with the Cybermen. Now my dreams were more likely to be of Agnetha, the blonde one from ABBA – and these imaginings were taking on a whole new narrative.

Sharon Burgess had changed too. It was never the same after the Lord Mayor's Show. She never did win my big brother's affections, but I let her go. (Well, to be honest, she chucked me shortly after, and then she cancelled her *Bunty*.) Now Sharon got *Jackie* and was going out with a wee lad who was taller than me and stacked shelves in the Co-op on a Saturday. This was a rung or two above the vocation of the humble paperboy. I survived, though. For a while, the nice ladies in the lingerie section of the Great Universal Club Book kept me going. Then my attention turned to new girlfriend opportunities. I found I couldn't decide between church youth-club girl, chemistry-class girl or girl-next-door girl. I was keeping my options open.

I still enjoyed being a paperboy, but the six-nightly commitment was seriously starting to get in the way of being a teenager. The end was inevitable. Of course, I couldn't just leave, though – I needed something better to move on to.

But then it happened: I was headhunted. I was approached by Leslie, the local bread man, and the Shankill's leading Orangeman. Leslie asked me to become a van boy – not in any ordinary bread van, but in the last Ormo Mini Shop in Northern Ireland! The Ormo Mini Shop was like a cross between an ordinary bread van and a caravan. You could walk inside: it was a proper shop on wheels.

This was promotion. How could I turn down such a tempting job offer? Most paperboys could only dream of an employment opportunity like this. I jumped at this chance for career advancement and accepted the job immediately. Working for Leslie would be a one-day-a-week job: Saturday mornings only, for five hours and at twice the money. It would be a daylight job all year round, and I would be inside the mobile shop and out of the rain at least half of the time. I wouldn't have to walk everywhere. No wee hoods would be up in time to try to rob me on a Saturday morning, especially with an adult on board. And I had heard you got free Paris buns.

But how was I going to break the bad news to Oul' Mac? I was sure he would be angry, and I was certain that Mrs Mac would be absolutely heartbroken. I considered a written letter of resignation, but I realised that was not Oul' Mac's preferred method of communication. So I decided I would tell him face to face and man to man. I would even give my employer one week's notice – not like other boys, who on their final day would simply tell him where he could stick his paper round.

When the momentous day of my resignation came, it started out like any other. Oul' Mac arrived in the new dirty van with my forty-eight *Belfast Telegraphs* as usual. He pulled on the handbrake with a screech and, with the engine still running, got out of the driver's seat, walked around the van in grumpy silence and opened up the rear doors to reveal a treasure trove of newspapers and glossy magazines. He then leapt into the rear of the van, cigarette in mouth, and dispensed the papers. I waited until the end of the paperboy queue that day. Oul' Mac must have realised something was amiss because I had earned first place in the queue long ago.

When the other paperboys had all gone, I finally spoke to my employer, as he was cutting the familiar tight white string on my batch of *Tellys*. I took such a deep breath that I inhaled some of his copious smoke.

'I'm leavin', Mr Mac. I'm sorry, I've got too much homework to do now and ... er, I'll be doing GCEs and, um ... there's nothing wrong with doin' the papers, and I go to clubs after school and can't get home in time to do a good job any more, ye know, and I don't want to let you down but I'm leavin' next week, I'll leave my paperbag into the shop next Saturday after the *Ulsters* and thanks for the job and I've got a Saturday job now instead ...' I spluttered incoherently.

A long concertina of ash fell from Oul' Mac's cigarette. For the first time ever, he patted me on the back, and his eyes sparkled a little.

'Aye, all right, wee lad,' he said.

I was a paperboy no more. My career had just taken off like *Thunderbird 3*. I was a breadboy now, so I was.